LAKESIDE SCHOOL
A Welcoming Place for Newcomers

Older students newly arrived in the U. S. face many challenges: a different culture, a different language, often even a completely different system of writing. Some may be attending school for the first time in their lives or reentering school after a long interruption. Others may have literacy skills in their native language. Although no two student profiles are alike, all newcomers bring a valuable set of language skills and a rich experiential base to your classroom, and they share similar aspirations: attaining fluency in English and achieving success alongside their peers.

It takes time and specialized instructional approaches to effectively integrate newly arrived older students into the mainstream of the American school system. Their immediate needs upon arrival are well known:

- They need to quickly develop a set of "survival" English language skills and vocabulary, to allow them to meet the simple everyday requirements of their new environment.

- They need to start reading and writing in English so that they can build the literacy skills so essential to their academic success.

- They may need to build self-esteem and confidence. Research shows that second-language acquisition occurs more smoothly and swiftly when students' affective filters are low. Use the strategies in the box at right to help your students feel "at home" more quickly.

The *Lakeside School* program meets the needs of newcomer students through an array of components that specifically and effectively address each of the points outlined above. Students follow Carlos, a student navigating through his first day at a new school, as he goes from class to class, meeting new situations and new people. In the course of following Carlos through his new experiences, students learn the basic language skills they will need to succeed in *their* new experiences.

For a look at the components that make up *Lakeside School*, please turn to pages T1b–T1c. An overview of the activities and skills covered in each lesson appears on pages T1h–T1k. We welcome you to *Lakeside School* and hope that it becomes a welcoming place for your newly arrived students as well.

Lower the Affective Filter!

- Affirm students' home language and culture. Acquire first-hand knowledge—check out movies, books, or music from the home culture; talk with community members; visit stores in the new immigrant community. Invite families to participate in activities that don't require English. Encourage newcomers to use their home language in narrating wordless books or creating their own books and storyboards.

- Pair bilingual peers with newcomers for a week or more. "Buddies" can eat lunch with newcomers and/or give a school tour. If this isn't possible, have an English-speaking volunteer be a newcomer's buddy.

- Create a nurturing classroom environment. Emphasize meaning over accuracy. Correct errors indirectly through modeling. Celebrate all efforts at producing English.

- Make progress visible. Many students expect instant English and become frustrated quickly. Save and share examples of students' earliest attempts at spoken and written English to illustrate their progress. Provide informal feedback—*Wow, your English is really improving. You have so much to say now!* Communicate successes to families.

Program Components

Student Book

The Student Book uses a picture-dictionary approach and natural conversations to teach:

- survival vocabulary, such as school locations and objects, numbers, food, and money
- language functions
- basic patterns and structures
- high-frequency words.

Posters

16 posters that present:

- Lakeside School scenes with vocabulary call-outs
- natural conversations and role-plays for trying out language.

CD and Tape

- Audio recordings contain readings and language-building activities for the conversations in the Student Book and the Posters.

Student Journal

The Student Journal provides opportunities to personalize learning to the student's own school and life. It features:

- extensive skills practice and repetition
- vocabulary building
- practice with English sounds and letters
- partner and small-group activities to promote language production.

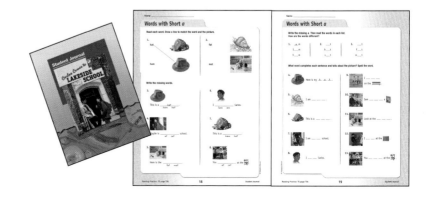

Carlos Comes to LAKESIDE SCHOOL

Teacher's Edition

HAMPTON-BROWN

Hampton-Brown
P.O. Box 223220
Carmel, California 93922
1–800–333–3510

Printed in the United States of America
0-7362-1298-1

06 07 08 09 10 10 9 8 7 6 5 4 3 2

ACKNOWLEDGMENTS
Every effort has been made to secure permission, but if any omissions have been made please let us know. We gratefully acknowledge the following permissions:

ZB Font Method Copyright © 1996 Zaner Bloser

Photographs

Art & Science: pT85, T90 © Art and Science Artville; **Artville:** pT6, T22, T23; **Digital Stock:** pT3, T85; **Digital Studios:** pT23; **Eyewire:** pT90 ©Eyewire; **Image Bank:** pT30 ©Karina Wang; **John Paul Endress:** pT90; **Liz Garza Williams:** pT3–T31, T84–T90, T93; **New Century Graphics:** pT23, T27, T31, T85; **Object Gear:** pT90; **PhotoDisc:** pT90 ©Ryan McVey; **Photo Edit:** pT30 ©Brian Haimer, pT31 ©Tony Freeman; **PictureQuest:** pT24 ©DigitalVision/Picture Quest, ©Don Farrall/Photo Disc/PictureQuest, ©Steve Mason/ PhotoDisc/PictureQuest, ©Corbis Images/PictureQuest, Koudis/PictureQuest; **Stone:** pT31 ©2000 Stone/Randy Wells

The High Point Development Team
Hampton-Brown extends special thanks to the following individuals and companies who contributed so much to the creation of this book.

Editorial: Janine Boylan, Lisa Cittadino, Shirleyann Costigan, Ramiro Ferrey, Tiina Kurvi, Dawn Liseth, Daphne Liu, Sherry Long, Guadalupe López, Jacalyn Mahler, Juan Quintana, Beth Sengel, Virginia Yeater, Lynn Yokoe, and Ink, Inc.

Design and Production: Debbie Saxton, Curtis Spitler, Cathy Revers, Deborah Miller, Donna Turner, J.R. Walker, Connie Delagarza, Davis Hernandez, Marcia Walker, Margaret Tisdale, Alex von Dallwitz, Russell Nemec, Jeri Gibson, Roger Rybkowski, Jana Abell, Lisa Baehr, Darius Detwiler, Raymond Hoffmeyer, Colette Nichol, Stephanie Rice, Alicia Sternberg, Debbie Wright Swisher, Andrea Erin Thompson, Erika Vinup, Chaos Factory & Associates, Ray Godfrey, Roy Neuhaus

Contents

Sound and Letter Transparencies

- 10 color transparencies for phonics instruction.

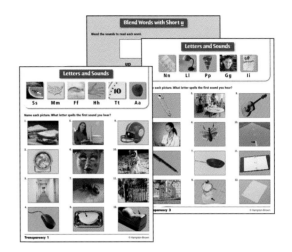

Letter Tiles

- Transparent tiles with uppercase and lowercase letters for word-building and blending activities on the overhead projector.

Word Tiles

- Transparent tiles for high-frequency-word instruction and sentence building
- Punctuation marks and blanks for cloze activities.

Teacher's Edition

Includes complete lesson plans along with:

- masters for creating letter cards to use in word-building and blending activities
- handwriting instruction and practice in both manuscript and cursive
- tests and guidelines for effective assessment.

Scope and Sequence

The following skills are taught in *Lakeside School*. Objectives for each lesson appear in the Activity Planner on pages T1h–T1k.

Concepts and Vocabulary

BASIC VOCABULARY

Actions

Body parts

Careers

Classroom activities

Classroom objects and school tools

Clothing

Colors

Commands

Days of the week

Food

Greetings and introductions

Library objects

Money

Months of the year

Numbers

Personal information

School locations and objects

School subjects

Science materials and processes

Shapes

Sickness and injury

Social courtesies

Sports

Telling time

Tools

Language Development and Communication

LANGUAGE FUNCTIONS

Ask and answer questions

Ask for and give information

Describe

Express feelings

Express likes and dislikes

Express needs, wants, and thoughts

Express social courtesies

Give and carry out commands

Listen actively

Repeat spoken language

Use the telephone

LANGUAGE PATTERNS AND STRUCTURES

Abbreviations

Basic sentence patterns

   A _____ is in the _____.

   Can you _____?

   Carlos _____. (noun + action verb)

   Do you like _____?

   Does _____?

   He/She has _____.

   Here is/are _____.

   How do they feel? They feel _____.

   How do you feel? I feel _____.

   How does he/she feel? He/she feels _____.

   I am _____.

   I can _____.

   I do not like _____.

   I have _____.

   I like _____.

   I like this/that/these/those _____.

   I need _____.

   I need to _____.

   I think _____.

   Is this _____?

   My _____ hurts/hurt.

   My name is _____.

   My phone number is _____.

   Point to _____.

   See you _____.

   Show me _____.

Language Development and Communication, continued

Some _____ are in the _____.

Some _____ are _____. /A _____ is _____.

They have _____.

This/That is _____.

What is _____?

What is in the _____?

What is this/that?

What time is it? It is _____. It is time for _____.

Where is _____?

Which do you like?

Who is _____?

Will you _____?

You can _____.

Capitalization (at the beginning of sentences)

Nouns

    Plurals with -s

    Singular

Sentences

    Declarative

    Exclamatory

    Imperative

    Interrogative

    Negative

    Statements with infinitives

Punctuation

    Exclamation mark

    Period

    Question mark

Verbs

    Modals (can)

    Present tense

    Singular and plural

    Subject-verb agreement

Reading

Develop phonemic awareness

Associate letters and sounds

    Consonants

    Short vowels

Blend sounds to decode words

Recognize high frequency words

a, am, an, and, answer, are, around, at, book, both, boy, call, can, day, do, does, don't, feel, food, for, get, girl, give, good, great, group, has, have, he, help, here, how, I, in, is, it, later, letters, like, little, look, me, my, name, need, night, no, not, number, of, old, on, picture, play, point, put, read, school, see, she, show, some, soon, take, that, the, them, these, they, things, think, this, those, time, to, tomorrow, too, very, we, what, where, which, who, will, with, work, write, yes, year, you, your

Listening

Representing

Speaking

Viewing

Writing

Statements

Questions

Exclamations

Assessment and Pacing

Assessment

LANGUAGE ACQUISITION ASSESSMENT

Identifies Performance Assessment opportunities in each unit and offers scoring rubrics to monitor students' progress through the stages of language proficiency. For detailed directions, see pages T78–T79. The test appears on pages T82–T83.

POSTTEST IN STANDARDIZED TEST FORMAT

The multiple-choice section of this test measures students' cumulative understanding of skills and language. A section with writing prompts measures students' progress in writing skills and fluency. For detailed directions, see pages T80–T81. The test appears on pages T84–T93.

Pacing Options

Each of the 56 lessons will take about one 55-minute period, so that the program can be completed in about 12 weeks. If students spend more than one period per day in *Lakeside School,* the program can be completed more quickly. Or choose options from the Reaching All Students panel to provide additional reinforcement that will extend the time for each lesson.

Carlos Comes to Lakeside School

LAKESIDE
TEACHER'S EDITION
PAGES

T2–T3

Cover

LESSON 1 pages T2–T3
Vocabulary
　Numbers

T4–T5
T5a–T5b

Pages 4–5

LESSON 2 page T4
Vocabulary
　School Locations and Objects

LESSON 3 page T5
Vocabulary
　Greeting and Introductions
Functions
　Give Information
　Express Social Courtesies
Patterns and Structures
　This is _____ .
　I am _____ .

LESSON 4 pages T5a–T5b
High Frequency Words
　am, I, is, school, the, this, you

T6–T7
T7a–T7b

Pages 6–7

LESSON 5 page T6
Vocabulary
　Classroom Objects and School Tools
Function
　Ask and Answer Questions
Patterns and Structures
　Is this _____ ?
　This is _____ .

LESSON 6 page T7
Vocabulary
　Greetings and Introductions
Function
　Express Social Courtesies
Patterns and Structures
　This is _____ .

LESSON 7 page T7a
High Frequency Words
　a, an, here, my, no, yes

LESSON 8 page T7b
Phonics
　Letters and Sounds: *Ss, Mm, Ff, Hh, Tt, Aa*

T8–T9
T9a–T9b

Pages 8–9

LESSON 9 page T8
Vocabulary
　School Locations

LESSON 10 page T9
Functions
　Express Social Courtesies
　Ask Questions
Patterns and Structures
　Where is _____ ?

LESSON 11 page T9a
High Frequency Words
　at, it, look, of, on, see, show, where

LESSON 12 page T9b
Phonics
　Blending: Words with short *a*

T10–T11
T11a–T11b

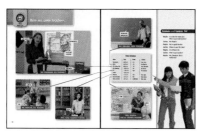

Pages 10–11

LESSON 13 page T10
Vocabulary
    School Subjects
    Telling Time
Function
    Give Information
Patterns and Structures
    What time is it?
    It is _____ .
    It is time for _____ .

LESSON 14 page T11
Functions
    Ask and Answer Questions
    Give Information
Patterns and Structures
    Where is _____ ?
    Who is _____ ?
    Here is _____ .
    Here are _____ .

LESSON 15 page T11a
High Frequency Words
    are, good, he, she, some, time, who, your

LESSON 16 page T11b
Phonics
    Letters and Sounds: *Nn, Ll, Pp, Gg, Ii*

T12–T13
T13a–T13b

Pages 12–13

LESSON 17 page T12
Vocabulary
    Classroom Activities

LESSON 18 page T13
Vocabulary
    Shapes
    Commands
Functions
    Give and Carry Out Commands
Patterns and Structures
    Show me _____ .
    Point to _____ .

LESSON 19 page T13a
High Frequency Words
    answer, point, read, to, with, work, write

LESSON 20 page T13b
Phonics
    Blending: Words with short *i*

T14–T15
T15a–T15b

Pages 14–15

LESSON 21 page T14
Vocabulary
    School Objects and Personnel
    Personal Information
Function
    Give Personal Information
Patterns and Structures
    My name is _____ .
    My phone number is _____ .

LESSON 22 page T15
Functions
    Ask for Information
    Express Needs
Patterns and Structures
    Where is _____ ?
    What is _____ ?
    I need to _____ .

LESSON 23 page T15a
High Frequency Words
    call, name, need, number, to, what

LESSON 24 page T15b
Phonics
    Letters and Sounds: *Rr, Dd, Cc, Vv, Oo*

T16–T17
T17a–T17b

Pages 16–17

LESSON 25 page T16
Vocabulary
    Library Objects
Function
    Ask for and Give Information
Patterns and Structures
    What is in the _____ ?
    A _____ is in the _____ .
    Some _____ are in the _____ .

LESSON 26 page T17
Functions
    Express Likes
    Ask and Answer Questions

LESSON 26, continued
Patterns and Structures
    Do you like _____ ?
    I like _____ .
    Will you _____ ?
    Does _____ ?

LESSON 27 page T17a
High Frequency Words
    do, does, for, help, in, like, me, picture, will

LESSON 28 page T17b
Phonics
    Blending: Words with short *o*

LAKESIDE
TEACHER'S EDITION
PAGES

T18–T19
T19a–T19b

Pages 18–19

LESSON 29 page T18
Vocabulary
    Sports
Function
    Express Likes
Patterns and Structures
    I like _____ .

LESSON 30 page T19
Function
    Ask and Answer Questions
Patterns and Structures
    Can you _____ ?
    I can _____ .
    You can _____ .

LESSON 31 page T19a
High Frequency Words
    around, can, play, too, we

LESSON 32 page T19b
Phonics
    Letters and Sounds: *Jj, Bb, Ww, Kk, Ee*

T20–T21
T21a–T21b

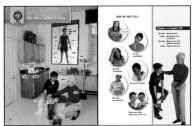

Pages 20–21

LESSON 33 page T20
Vocabulary
    Body Parts
Function
    Give Information
Patterns and Structures
    He/She has _____ .
    I/They have _____ .

LESSON 34 page T21
Functions
    Ask and Answer Questions
    Express Feelings

LESSON 34, continued
Patterns and Structures
    How do you/they feel?
    How does he/she feel?
    I/They feel _____ .
    He/She feels _____ .
    My _____ hurts.

LESSON 35 page T21a
High Frequency Words
    feel, has, have, how, put, they

LESSON 36 page T21b
Phonics
    Blending: Words with short *e*

T22–T23
T23a–T23b

Pages 22–23

LESSON 37 page T22
Vocabulary
    Food
Function
    Express Likes and Dislikes
Patterns and Structures
    I like _____ .
    I do not like _____ .

LESSON 38 page T23
Vocabulary
    Money

LESSON 38, continued
Function
    Ask for and Give Information
Patterns and Structures
    What is this/that?
    This/That is _____ .

LESSON 39 page T23a
High Frequency Words
    and, don't, food, not, that

LESSON 40 page T23b
Writing
    Write a Statement

T24–T25
T25a–T25b

Pages 24–25

LESSON 41 page T24
Vocabulary
    Science Materials and Processes

LESSON 42 page T25
Function
    Express Needs and Thoughts
Patterns and Structures
    I need _____ .
    I think _____ .

LESSON 43 page T25a
High Frequency Words
    give, take, think

LESSON 44 page T25b
Phonics
    Letters and Sounds: *Zz, Yy, Uu, QU qu, Xx*

T26–T27
T27a–T27b

Pages 26–27

LESSON 45 page T26
Vocabulary
   Clothing
   Colors

LESSON 46 page T27
Function
   Ask and Answer Questions
Patterns and Structures
   Which _____ *do you like?*
   I like this/that _____ *.*
   I like these/those _____ *.*

LESSON 47 page T27a
High Frequency Words
   both, get, little, old, them,
   these, things, those, very, which

LESSON 48 page T27b
Phonics
   Blending: Words with short *u*

T28–T29
T29a–T29b

Pages 28–29

LESSON 49 page T28
Vocabulary
   Days of the Week
   Abbreviations for Days
      of the Week

LESSON 50 page T29
Function
   Express Social Courtesies
Patterns and Structures
   See you _____ *.*

LESSON 51 page T29a
High Frequency Words
   great, later, soon, tomorrow

LESSON 52 page T29b
Writing
   Write a Question

T30–T31
T31a–T31b

Pages 30–31

LESSON 53 page T30
Vocabulary
   Months of the Year

LESSON 54 page T31
Vocabulary
   Action Verbs
Function
   Describe Actions
Patterns and Structures
   Present Tense Verbs

LESSON 55 page T31a
High Frequency Words
   book, boy, day, girl, group, letters,
   night, year

LESSON 56 page T31b
Writing
   Write an Exclamation

BASIC VOCABULARY AND LANGUAGE DEVELOPMENT

OBJECTIVES

Reading and Learning Strategies:
Activate Prior Knowledge; Relate to
Personal Experience; Build Background

Viewing: Interpret a Visual Image

LEARN ABOUT LAKESIDE SCHOOL

1 **Introduce Lakeside School** Read
the title on the cover and point to the
picture of Carlos. Explain: *This book
tells about a boy named Carlos. He is
new at Lakeside School.*

Point out the sign on the building:
Lakeside School. Tell students that the
picture shows Carlos outside his new
school. Explain that he is meeting a
girl named Maylin, who will help him
through his first day.

2 **Preview the Book** Point out the
clock on page 4 and explain: *Carlos's
story starts at the beginning of the
school day. We will go with Carlos to his
classes. We will see what he does
during the day. These clocks tell us what
time it is.* Have students page through
the book to point out the clock on
each left-hand page. Then read aloud
the sentence that appears next to the
clock and allow students time to look
through the photographs.

REACHING ALL STUDENTS

HOME CONNECTION

At Home with Numbers To reinforce
number concepts, encourage students
to take home completed **Student
Journal** pages 4 and 5. Students can
read the number words aloud to
family members. Then students and
family members can list or draw
home items containing numerals.
Students can write the number words
and bring their lists or drawings to
school to share.

Carlos Comes to LAKESIDE SCHOOL

85 LAKE AVENUE

Language Development
NUMBERS

Play number bingo. Show students how to make a 5 x 5 grid and have them copy numbers from **Student Journal** page 4 onto their grids. Call out numbers and have students mark them off on their grids until someone fills a row, a column, or a diagonal. Invite the student who wins the first round to call the numbers for the second round. As a variation, use only numbers from 1–50 or 51–100.

BASIC VOCABULARY AND LANGUAGE DEVELOPMENT

OBJECTIVES

Functions:
Listen Actively; Repeat Spoken Language
Concepts and Vocabulary: Numbers

USE NUMBERS

1 **Introduce Numbers** Point out the number 85 in the address for Lakeside School. Tell students that Carlos will see and use many numbers at school. Brainstorm places to find numbers: room numbers, schedules, clocks, buses, uniforms.

2 **Identify Numbers** Use **Student Journal** page 4 or make a chart to teach numbers and number words:

1 one	25 twenty-five
2 two	26 twenty-six
3 three	27 twenty-seven
4 four	28 twenty-eight
5 five	29 twenty-nine
6 six	30 thirty
7 seven	40 forty
8 eight	50 fifty
9 nine	60 sixty
10 ten	70 seventy
11 eleven	80 eighty
12 twelve	90 ninety
13 thirteen	100 one hundred
14 fourteen	101 one hundred one
15 fifteen	110 one hundred ten
16 sixteen	120 one hundred twenty
17 seventeen	130 one hundred thirty
18 eighteen	140 one hundred forty
19 nineteen	150 one hundred fifty
20 twenty	160 one hundred sixty
21 twenty-one	170 one hundred seventy
22 twenty-two	180 one hundred eighty
23 twenty-three	190 one hundred ninety
24 twenty-four	200 two hundred

Point to each number, say it, and have students echo-read. Next, call out numbers at random and have students point to them.

▶ **Student Journal** pages 4, 5

CLOSE AND ASSESS

Make two sets of cards, one with numerals and one with number words. Have students match the cards and say the numbers.

BASIC VOCABULARY AND LANGUAGE DEVELOPMENT

OBJECTIVES

Concepts and Vocabulary:
❶ School Locations and Objects
Viewing: Interpret a Visual Image
Representing: Drawing

USE NAMES OF SCHOOL LOCATIONS AND OBJECTS

1 **Look at the Photographs** Point out the clock and explain: *It's 8:20 a.m. Time for school! Carlos is just going in. These photos show what Lakeside School looks like.*

Have students look at the main building on page 4. Say: *This is the front of the school. It is the outside of the building.* Point to each labeled item as you read its name. As you discuss the second photo, explain: *The entrance hall is inside the school. This is what you see when you go in the front door.*

Repeat the procedure with the photos on page 5. Explain that both photos show areas outside.

2 **Sketch a School Building** If possible, lead the class outside to face the main building of your school. Have students sketch the exterior in the space provided on page 6 of the **Student Journal**. (If it is not possible to go outside, students can sketch from memory.) Encourage them to include details such as windows, doors, and steps.

3 **Label the Sketches** In class, have students use the photos on this page as a model for labeling their own sketches. Supply specific words for your school, as necessary.

▶ **Student Journal** page 6

CLOSE AND ASSESS

Call out school locations and objects for students to identify on their sketches.

Time:
8:20 a.m.

This is Lakeside School.

This is the main building.

window
flag
front door
steps

This is the entrance hall.

light
bulletin board
clock
room number
student
door
hallway

122

4

REACHING ALL STUDENTS

Vocabulary
SCHOOL LOCATIONS

Sort Photos Take snapshots of several locations and objects around your school. Invite volunteers to label the items they know. Then work together to arrange the photos into two categories: *Inside the School* and *Outside the School*.

Inside the School	Outside the School
light	street
clock	field

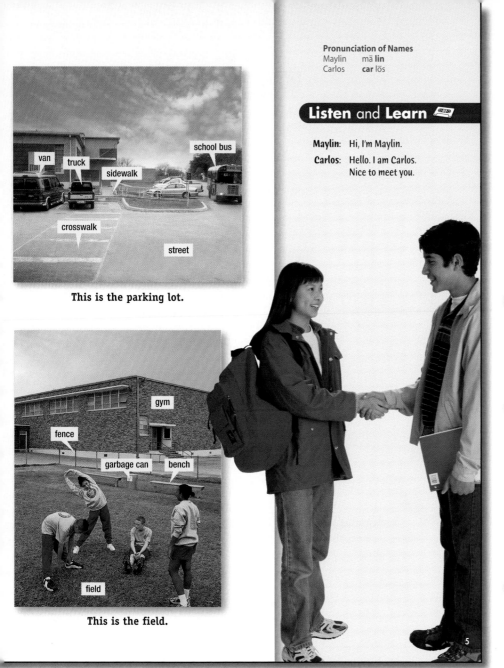

This is the parking lot.

This is the field.

Listen and Learn

Maylin: Hi, I'm Maylin.
Carlos: Hello. I am Carlos. Nice to meet you.

Language Development

GIVE INFORMATION

Divide the class into small groups and have the members share their sketches from **Student Journal** page 6. The group combines the information from each sketch to create a large, labeled drawing of the main school building. Provide the sentence frame: *This is the ____.* Then invite group members to act as tour guides to give information about the building: *This is the front door of our school.*

BASIC VOCABULARY AND LANGUAGE DEVELOPMENT

OBJECTIVES

Functions: Listen Actively; Repeat Spoken Language; Give Information; Express Social Courtesies

Concepts and Vocabulary: Greetings and Introductions

Patterns and Structures: ❶ *I am ____.;* ❶ *This is ____.*

Speaking: Introductions

GIVE INFORMATION

1 **Introduce the Pattern:** *This is ____.* Read aloud the captions. Then use the pattern to tell about objects on these pages: *This is the flag.* Have students describe the features in your classroom: *This is the door.*

2 **Take a School Tour** As you walk, pause for students to check off and label on **Student Journal** page 7 the objects they see. Provide vocabulary for additional items. Back in class, have volunteers tell about the items they found.

▶ **Student Journal** page 7

EXPRESS SOCIAL COURTESIES

3 **Introduce the Pattern:** *I am ____.* Play the "Listen and Learn" conversation on the **Lakeside Language Tape/CD.** Students will listen twice to the conversation, then echo the lines, and chime in on Carlos's part. Ask volunteers to role-play the conversation.

4 **Practice Introductions** Organize students into an Inside-Outside Circle (see page T94). Students in the inside circle say: *Hi, I'm ____.* Students in the outside circle say: *Hello. I am ____. Nice to meet you.* Rotate the circles for more practice.

CLOSE AND ASSESS

Have one partner point to an item on pages 4–5; the other describes it with this pattern: *This is ____.*

LANGUAGE AND LITERACY: HIGH FREQUENCY WORDS

OBJECTIVES

Learning to Read:
❶ Recognize High Frequency Words

INTRODUCE

1 **Learn New Words** Place a word and its letter tiles on the screen as you work through the Strategy for Learning a New Word. For example, for *this,* say:

1. *First, look at the word.* (Display the word tile for *this*.)

2. *Now listen to the word:* this, this.

3. *Listen to the word in a sentence:* What school is this? This is Lakeside School. *What does the word* this *mean? It means "the one we are talking about."*

4. *Say the word after me:* this.

5. *Spell the word:* t-h-i-s. (As you say each letter, place the corresponding letter tile below the word tile. Have students spell the word again in unison as you point to each tile.)

6. *Say the word again:* this.

Repeat the process for each new word. Good sentences for the third step are:

• What **is** your name?
• Read **the** book.
• We go to **school**.
• **I** like our class.
• I **am** the teacher.
• **You** are students.

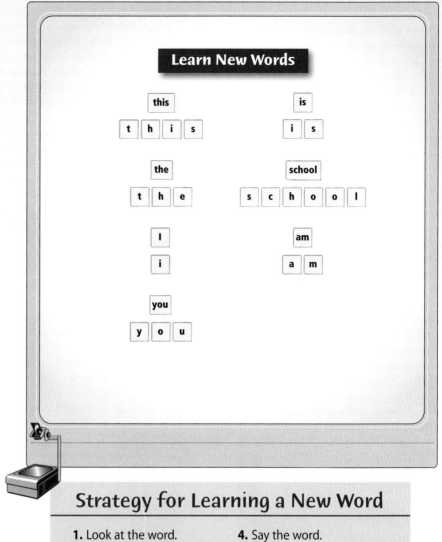

Strategy for Learning a New Word

1. Look at the word.
2. Listen to the word.
3. Listen to the word in a sentence.
4. Say the word.
5. Spell the word.
6. Say the word again.

REACHING ALL STUDENTS

Reading Fluency
RECOGNIZE HIGH FREQUENCY WORDS

To build automaticity with the new words, create a classroom word chart for display throughout the year. First, demonstrate printing each new word on a card. After the first word or two, print just the first letter and have students tell you the next. Model how to post a card on the chart by the first letter in the word. Have volunteers post the rest.

Students can use the classroom chart to practice together. For example:

• One student can say a word for another to find on the chart.
• Partners can match their word cards against the words on the chart.
• Small groups can challenge one another in hunts; for example, find three words with three letters each.

Aa	Ee	Ii	Mm	Qq	Uu
Bb	Ff	Jj	Nn	Rr	Vv

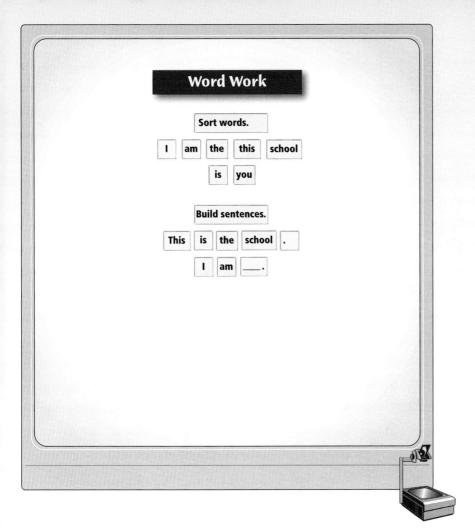

Word Work

Sort words.

| I | am | the | this | school |

| is | you |

Build sentences.

| This | is | the | school | . |

| I | am | ___ . |

2 Sort Words Place the direction tile on the screen and then place the word tiles in a random arrangement. Have students sort the words by the number of letters. Ask: *Which word has one letter?* (I) *Which words have two letters?* (am, is), etc. As students name the words, arrange them in groups. Finally, lead a choral reading of the words in each group.

3 Build Sentences Place the direction tile and then the word tiles on the screen to create the sentences shown. As you place each word, say it. Explain the placement of the periods: *This sentence tells something, so we use a period at the end.*

Model reading the text and filling in the blank: *This is the school. I am* [your name]. Have partners read the sentences aloud, inserting their names.

APPLY

4 Read New Words Have students apply the skill by turning to pages 4–5 and finding each of the new words in the text.

▶ **Student Journal** page 8

CLOSE AND ASSESS

Place the high frequency words one at a time on the screen. Call on volunteers to read them; have the group repeat them.

Multi-Level Strategies
LANGUAGE DEVELOPMENT

PRELITERATE The sentences you built in Step 3 can be used to check students' command of basic print concepts and classroom vocabulary (*word, letter, point,* etc.). Display the sentences on the overhead as shown. Then ask students to:

• count the number of words in each sentence.

• point to the first word in the sentence.

• point to the first letter in that word.

• show where to start reading again after the first sentence.

If students have difficulty with the tasks, use a classroom book with simple text to develop these concepts of print as well as the basic vocabulary students will need to participate in instruction.

BASIC VOCABULARY AND LANGUAGE DEVELOPMENT

OBJECTIVES

Functions: Listen Actively; Repeat Spoken Language; Ask and Answer Questions
Concepts and Vocabulary:
❶ Classroom Objects; ❶ School Tools
Patterns and Structures:
❶ *Here is* _____*.; Is this* _____*?*
Viewing: Interpret a Visual Image

USE NAMES OF CLASSROOM OBJECTS AND SCHOOL TOOLS

1 Introduce the Pattern: *Here is* _____*.*
Point to the clock and say: *Now it is 8:30. Carlos is in class. There are many things that he can use.* Use the pattern to introduce each classroom object: *Here is a pencil. I use a pencil to write.*

Turn to **Student Journal** page 9 and model how to complete the diminishing sentences in the first column. Have partners complete the remaining sentences.

▶ **Student Journal** page 9

ASK AND ANSWER QUESTIONS

2 Introduce the Patterns:
Is this _____*?* **and**
This is _____*.* Play the "Listen and Learn" conversation on the **Lakeside Language Tape/CD**. Students listen to the conversation as they follow along, and then echo it. On a last reading, they chime in with Carlos.

Then turn to **Student Journal** page 10 and help students prepare game spinners. Invite volunteers to model the game, then have small groups play together to practice the skill.

▶ **Student Journal** page 10

CLOSE AND ASSESS

Have one partner hold up a school tool and ask a question with the pattern *Is this* _____*?* The other partner answers with a statement: *This is* _____*.*

Here is a classroom.

a wall

a bookcase

a bookshelf
a window
a pencil sharpener

a book

paper

a notebook

SCHOOL SUPPLIES

a stapler

an eraser   a pencil   a pen   a highlighter   scissors

a ruler

a desk

Time: 8:30 a.m.

6

REACHING ALL STUDENTS

Vocabulary

CLASSROOM OBJECTS AND TOOLS

Labels, Labels Divide the classroom into several areas and assign a team to each area. Have each team identify the objects in their area and write the words on separate self-stick notes. The teams then trade their areas and notes and work together to affix the labels to the correct objects. Invite students to give information to the class: *This is a pencil sharpener.* Advanced students can tell more: *I use a pencil sharpener when my pencil is dull.*

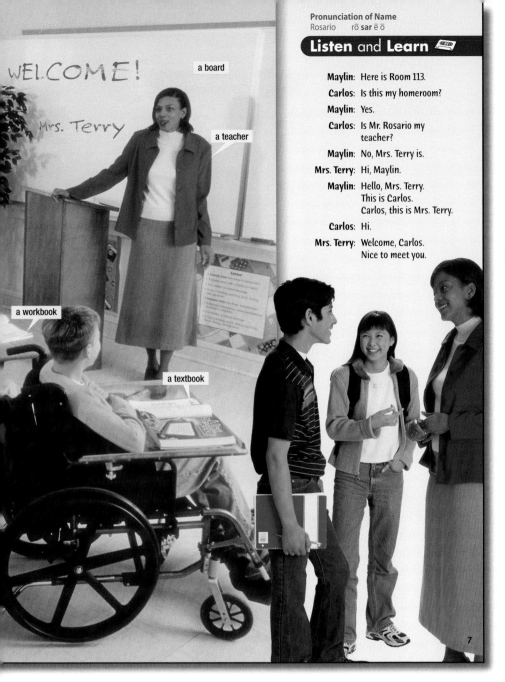

WELCOME!

Mrs. Terry

a board

a teacher

a workbook

a textbook

Pronunciation of Name
Rosario   rō **sar** ē ō

Listen and Learn

Maylin:	Here is Room 113.
Carlos:	Is this my homeroom?
Maylin:	Yes.
Carlos:	Is Mr. Rosario my teacher?
Maylin:	No, Mrs. Terry is.
Mrs. Terry:	Hi, Maylin.
Maylin:	Hello, Mrs. Terry. This is Carlos. Carlos, this is Mrs. Terry.
Carlos:	Hi.
Mrs. Terry:	Welcome, Carlos. Nice to meet you.

7

BASIC VOCABULARY AND LANGUAGE DEVELOPMENT

OBJECTIVES

Functions: Listen Actively; Repeat Spoken Language; Express Social Courtesies

Concepts and Vocabulary: Greetings and Introductions

Patterns and Structures: *This is _____.*

EXPRESS SOCIAL COURTESIES

1 Use Introductions Review the greetings from page 5: *hi, hello,* and *nice to meet you.* Then explain: *When you want two people to meet, you can gesture to one person and say: "This is ___."*

Replay the first reading of the conversation on the **Lakeside Language Tape/CD.** Have students listen for where Maylin introduces Carlos and Mrs. Terry. Invite them to repeat after you: *Carlos, this is Mrs. Terry.*

Side A

CD Track 2

2 Make Introductions Work together to match the speech balloons to the correct person on **Student Journal** page 11. Then make a chart to review words and phrases that are used in introductions. Have groups of three role-play one student introducing a new student to a teacher.

First Student:	Hi, _____. This is _____. _____, this is my friend _____.
New Student:	Hi, _____.
Teacher:	Welcome, _____. Nice to meet you.

▶ **Student Journal** page 11

CLOSE AND ASSESS

Have partners take turns introducing each other to you.

CULTURAL PERSPECTIVES

World Cultures: *Hello* **in Many Languages** Point out that every language has greetings. Invite students to teach the class how to say hello in languages they know. Then have the group make a poster with the title *"Hello" in Many Languages.* Invite students to add the names of their native languages and include the words and phrases they use to greet friends and family.

LANGUAGE AND LITERACY: HIGH FREQUENCY WORDS

OBJECTIVES

Learning to Read:
❶ Recognize High Frequency Words

INTRODUCE

1 Learn New Words Place a word and its letter tiles on the screen as you work through Strategy steps. For *yes*, say:

1. *First, look at the word.* (Display the word tile for *yes*.)

2. *Now listen to the word:* yes, yes.

3. *Listen to the word in a sentence:* Yes, this is an English class.

4. *Say the word after me:* yes.

5. *Spell the word:* y-e-s. (Say each letter as you place the tile. Point to each tile and have students spell the word.)

6. *Say the word again:* yes.

Repeat the process for the other words, using these context sentences:

- Is this **an** English class?
- **No**, this is homeroom.
- Is **my** teacher here?
- Yes. **Here** is the teacher.
- Here is **a** desk for you.

PRACTICE

2 Build Sentences Say each word as you place its tile on the screen: *Is this a _____? Is this an _____? Yes, this is _____ _____. No. This is _____ _____.* Model reading the text and filling in the blanks with classroom objects: *Is this a pen? No. This is an eraser.* Then have one partner ask the question; the other gives the answer.

APPLY

3 Read New Words Have students find the new words on pages 6–7.

▶ **Student Journal** page 12

CLOSE AND ASSESS

Display the words for students to read.

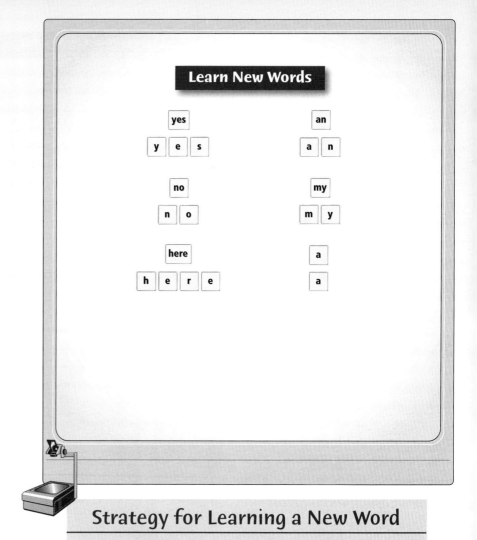

Strategy for Learning a New Word

1. Look at the word.
2. Listen to the word.
3. Listen to the word in a sentence.
4. Say the word.
5. Spell the word.
6. Say the word again.

REACHING ALL STUDENTS

Reading Fluency
RECOGNIZE HIGH FREQUENCY WORDS

To build automaticity with the new high frequency words:

- Display the words. Have pairs make a word card set. Then have them sort the cards by number of letters in each word. Volunteers can tell how many words have one, two, three, or four letters, and say the word or words.

- Partners can use the word cards to practice together and test each other. One holds up a card and the other reads the word. Have them add the previous set of words (page T5a) to the card set for review.

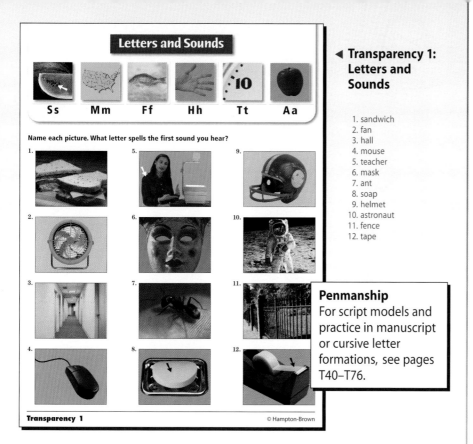

Letters and Sounds

Ss   Mm   Ff   Hh   Tt   Aa

Name each picture. What letter spells the first sound you hear?

1.   5.   9.

2.   6.   10.

3.   7.   11.

4.   8.   12.

Transparency 1   © Hampton-Brown

◄ **Transparency 1: Letters and Sounds**

1. sandwich
2. fan
3. hall
4. mouse
5. teacher
6. mask
7. ant
8. soap
9. helmet
10. astronaut
11. fence
12. tape

Penmanship
For script models and practice in manuscript or cursive letter formations, see pages T40–T76.

▼ **Script for Transparency 1**

Letters and Sounds

1. Develop Phonemic Awareness
Count Words in Sentences/Match Initial Sounds Say a sentence and have students count each word they hear: *Tom makes soup.* Then ask: *How many words are in this sentence?* (3) Repeat for: *Tom makes soup at home.* (5) Next, say: *Listen to these two words:* seed, soup. *Say the words with me:* seed, soup. *Do they begin with the same sound?* (yes) Repeat with these word pairs: *mud, hot; fast, fish; hit, home; ten, men; ask, apple; table, teacher.*

2. Associate Letters and Sounds
Learn Consonant Names, Sounds, and Formations Point to the seed on **Transparency 1**. Say: *This is a seed. Plants grow from seeds. Say* seed *with me:* seed. Then point to *Ss* and say: *This is capital* S, *and this is lowercase* s. *The letter* s *spells the first sound you hear in* seed. *The first sound is* /s/. *Say* /sss/ *with me:* /sss/. Point to the *s* and ask: *What is the letter? What is its sound?* Trace the *Ss* on the transparency as you explain how to form the letters and have students "write" the letters in the air. Repeat the process for *m, f, h,* and *t.* Then explain: *The letters* s, m, f, h, *and* t *are called* **consonants**—*they spell consonant sounds.*

Learn the Name, Sound, and Formation for the Vowel *Aa* Point to *Aa* and say: *This is the letter* a—*capital* A *and lowercase* a. *The letter* a *is a* **vowel**. Point to the apple and say: *Say* apple *with me:* apple. *Say its first sound:* /aaa/. *The sound* /aaa/ *is a vowel sound. When you say a vowel sound, you keep your mouth open and let the air flow out.* Try it: /aaa/. Then say: *The letter* a *spells the vowel sound* /a/ *you hear in* apple. Point to the *a* and ask: *What is the letter? What is its sound?* Then teach students how to form capital and lowercase *a*.

Practice Have students number a paper from 1–12. For Item 1, say: *What is in this picture? Let's say the word and then its first sound:* sandwich, /sss/. *What letter spells* /sss/ *as in* sandwich? *That's right,* s. Point to the *Ss* on the transparency. Have students write a capital and lowercase *s* by Item 1 on their papers. Repeat the process for Items 2–12.

LANGUAGE AND LITERACY: PHONICS

OBJECTIVES

Learning to Read: Build Oral Vocabulary; Develop Phonemic Awareness; ❶ Associate Letters and Sounds

TEACH LETTERS AND SOUNDS

1 **Build Oral Vocabulary** Display Transparency 1. Play "I Spy." For example, for Item 10, say:

• *I spy an astronaut. An astronaut wears a special suit and travels in space. This astronaut is on the moon.*

When students find the astronaut, say: *Yes,* **this is an astronaut** (point). Repeat for the other words.

2 **Develop Phonemic Awareness** Remove the transparency and work through Step 1 of the script.

3 **Associate Letters and Sounds** Display Transparency 1 again. Work through Step 2 of the script.

▶ **Student Journal** pages 13, 14

CLOSE AND ASSESS

Say the words *soap, hall, apple, mask, tape, fence* one at a time. Have the group write the letter that stands for the first sound in the word on a card and hold it up.

Review and Reteaching
PHONEMIC AWARENESS AND PHONICS

• **Match Initial Sounds** Say a sound and two words. Ask students to say which word begins with the sound you name. Some sounds and words to use are: /s/ *fan, soap;* /m/ *mask, hall;* /f/ *tape, fence;* /h/ *hand, mouse;* /t/ *tape, girl.*

• **Match Letters and Sounds** Give one letter card for *s, m, f, h, t,* or *a* (see pages T33–T38) to six students. Have the others each draw a picture from the transparency. Then students form groups to match the letters to the first sound in the picture names.

BASIC VOCABULARY AND LANGUAGE DEVELOPMENT

USE NAMES OF SCHOOL LOCATIONS

1 **View the Map** Explain: *This is a map of Lakeside School. It shows the location of all the rooms in the building.*

Point out the room labeled "library" on the map. Then direct students' attention to the photo of the library on page 9. Ask: *What do you see in the library?* (books, students) *What do students do there?* (read, study, research) Continue to make connections between the map locations and the photos.

2 **Start Maps of Your School** Begin by drawing a large outline of your school floor plan on a chart, explaining: *We can draw a map of our school, too. Here is the main building.* Divide your outline into rooms. Then have students copy the map onto page 15 of the **Student Journal**.

3 **Go on a Tour and Complete the School Maps** Conduct a tour of the places in your school. Have students label the locations you visit on their maps, using the vocabulary in the box on the **Student Journal** page. Supply additional place names for your particular school, as necessary.

▶ **Student Journal** page 15

Time: 8:40 a.m.

This is a map of the school.

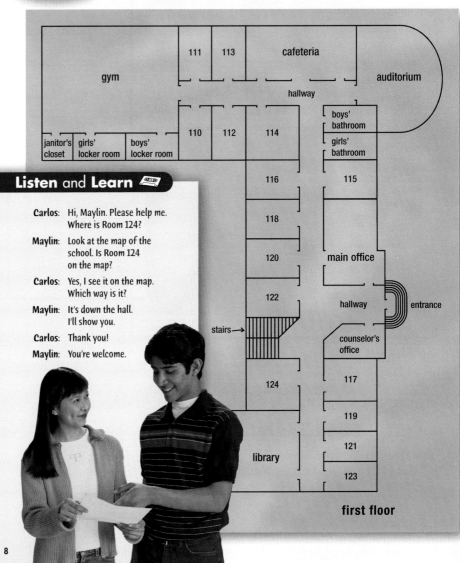

Listen and **Learn**

Carlos: Hi, Maylin. Please help me. Where is Room 124?

Maylin: Look at the map of the school. Is Room 124 on the map?

Carlos: Yes, I see it on the map. Which way is it?

Maylin: It's down the hall. I'll show you.

Carlos: Thank you!

Maylin: You're welcome.

8

REACHING ALL STUDENTS

Vocabulary
SCHOOL LOCATIONS

Map Puzzles Have small groups choose a group member's map to turn into a puzzle. Make a copy of the map and cut it apart so that each room is one piece. Groups should mix up the pieces and then work to put them back together. Encourage students to name each room as they place it in the puzzle.

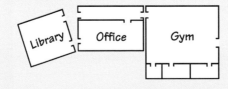

WHERE IS IT ON THE MAP?

THE MAIN OFFICE

THE COUNSELOR'S OFFICE

THE LIBRARY

THE GIRLS' BATHROOM

THE AUDITORIUM

THE CAFETERIA

9

BASIC VOCABULARY AND LANGUAGE DEVELOPMENT

OBJECTIVES

Functions: Listen Actively; Repeat Spoken Language; Express Social Courtesies; Ask Questions

Patterns and Structures:
❶ *Where is _____?*

EXPRESS SOCIAL COURTESIES

1 **Use *Please, Thank You, and You're Welcome***

Side A
CD Track 3

Play the "Listen and Learn" conversation on the **Lakeside Language Tape/CD**. Students will listen twice to the conversation. On the second reading, have them raise their hands when they hear the words *please, thank you,* and *you're welcome.* As the tape continues, students will echo lines and then chime in on Carlos's part. Afterwards, use the terms in a simple role-play with a volunteer: *Please give me a pencil. Okay. Thank you. You're welcome.*

ASK QUESTIONS

2 **Introduce the Pattern: *Where is _____?*** Read what Carlos says first on page 8. Then say: *When you need to find out where something is, ask a question with* Where.

Model with the pictures on page 9: *Where is the main office?* Challenge the group to ask more questions about places and objects in your school. Collect the questions in a chart.

Where is _____?
Where is the gym?
Where is the nurse's office?

▶ **Student Journal** page 16

CLOSE AND ASSESS

Have partners work together to ask questions: one partner points to a location on page 9 and the other asks where it is.

Language Development
ASK QUESTIONS

Have students use the map of their school that they made in Lesson 9. In an Inside-Outside Circle (see Cooperative Learning Structures, page T94), students can ask each other questions about where places are on the map. Provide this question starter:

Where is _____?

To answer, students point to the location on the map. Then the inside circle rotates and new partners repeat the process.

Language Development **T9**

LANGUAGE AND LITERACY: HIGH FREQUENCY WORDS

OBJECTIVES

Learning to Read:
❶ Recognize High Frequency Words

INTRODUCE

1 Learn New Words Place a word and its letter tiles on the screen as you work through the Strategy steps. For example, for *of,* say:

1. *First, look at the word.* (Display the word tile for *of.*)

2. *Now listen to the word:* of, of.

3. *Listen to the word in a sentence:* This is a map of the school.

4. *Say the word after me:* of.

5. *Spell the word:* o-f. (Say each letter as you place the tile. Point to each tile and have students spell the word.)

6. *Say the word again:* of.

Repeat the process for the other words, using these context sentences:

• Please **show** me the map.
• **Where** is Room 124?
• Is Room 124 **on** the map?
• Yes, **look at** the map.
• Now I **see it** on the map.

PRACTICE

2 Build Sentences Say each word as you place its tile on the screen: *Where is the _____? I see it on the _____.* Model reading the text and filling in the blanks with classroom objects: *Where is the book? I see it on the table.* Then have one partner ask the question; the other gives the answer.

APPLY

3 Read New Words Have students find the new words on pages 8–9.

▶ **Student Journal** page 17

CLOSE AND ASSESS

Display the words one at a time for students to read.

Learn New Words

of	show
o f	s h o w

where	on
w h e r e	o n

look	at
l o o k	a t

see	it
s e e	i t

Strategy for Learning a New Word

1. Look at the word.
2. Listen to the word.
3. Listen to the word in a sentence.
4. Say the word.
5. Spell the word.
6. Say the word again.

REACHING ALL STUDENTS

Reading Fluency
RECOGNIZE HIGH FREQUENCY WORDS

To build automaticity with the new high frequency words:

• Have a volunteer look at the classroom chart of words, choose a word, and begin spelling it slowly. The rest of the group should try to guess the word in as few letters as possible.

• Have students list the new and review words by number of letters, on a chart like the one shown. Ask questions about the lists; for example: *Which list has the most words in it? How would you arrange each list in alphabetical order?*

1	2	3	4	5	6
I	is	the	this	where	school
a	am	you	here		
	an	yes	look		
	my	see	show		
	no				
	of				
	at				
	it				
	on				

Blend Words with Short <u>a</u>

Blend the sounds to read each word.

am	at	at
Sam	hat	fat
ham	sat	mat

Read each word. Which picture goes with the word?

1. hat
2. ham
3. mat

A.   B.   C.

◀ **Transparency 2: Blending**

Penmanship
For script models and practice in writing words in manuscript or cursive with correct letter spacing, see pages T40–T76.

Materials
Letter tiles for:

a	f	h	m

s	S	t

▼ **Script for Transparency 2**

Blend Words with Short *a*

1. Develop Phonemic Awareness
Match Initial Sounds/Match Final Sounds Say: *Listen to these two words:* at, am. *Say the words with me:* at, am. *The first sound in these words is the same:* /aaa/. *Now listen to these two words:* an, it. *Say the words with me:* an, it. *Is the first sound in each word the same?* (no) *Continue with word pairs* Sam, sat; ham, hat; fat, mat; at, hat. *Then say: Now listen to these two words:* hot, mat. *Say the words with me:* hot, mat. *They end with the same sound:* /t/. *Here are two more words:* ham, hat. *Say the words with me:* ham, hat. *Is the last sound in each word the same?* (no) *Continue with word pairs* hit, cat; pass, bus; ham, dot; if, is.

2. Blend Sounds to Read Words
Model Set letter tile *a* at the left in the box on **Transparency 2** and letter tile *m* at the right. Point to *a* and say: *The sound for this letter is* /aaa/. *As you say the sound, slide* a *next to* m, *and then put your finger under* m. *Say: I can blend the sound* /aaa/ *with the sound of the letter* m: /aaammm/. *Now I am going to say the word fast:* am. *Summarize: You can blend sounds like this to read a word. Just say the sound for the first letter, and blend it into the sound for the next letter.* Demonstrate again: Point to *a* and say: *Say the sound for* a *with me:* /aaa/. Repeat for *m:* /mmm/. *Then slide a finger below the letters* am *and say: Help me blend the two sounds:* /aaammm/. *Now let's say the word:* am. Then leave *am* at the right in the box, add letter tile *S* at the left, and repeat the process to read *Sam.* Remove the *S* and repeat the process to read *ham.*

Practice Have students read the words *am, Sam,* and *ham* below the box. Then repeat Model and Practice for the other two word sets.

3. Match Words and Pictures
Point to Item 1. Say: *Let's read this word.* Slide a finger slowly under the letters to lead students in sounding out the word: /haaat/, hat. Then say: *Which of these pictures—A, B, or C—shows a hat?* (B) Repeat the process for Items 2 and 3.

LANGUAGE AND LITERACY: PHONICS

OBJECTIVES

Learning to Read: Build Oral Vocabulary; Develop Phonemic Awareness; Blend Sounds to Decode Words

TEACH BLENDING

1 **Build Oral Vocabulary** Display Transparency 2. Use *am, at, sat,* and *fat* in sentences to build meaning:

• *I* **am** (your name). *You are* **at** *your desks. You* **sat** *there yesterday. If you eat too much, you will get* **fat**.

Use the pictures to develop the meaning of the words *ham, hat,* and *mat.* For example:

• *This is a* **mat**. *A* **mat** *is soft. It is like a cushion. Gymnasts practice on a* **mat**.

2 **Develop Phonemic Awareness** Remove the transparency and work through Step 1 of the script.

3 **Blend Sounds to Read Words** Display Transparency 2 again. Work through Steps 2 and 3 of the script.

▶ **Student Journal** pages 18, 19

CLOSE AND ASSESS

Display *hat, sat, ham,* and *fat.* Have students identify the sound of each letter and blend the sounds to read the word.

Review and Reteaching
PHONEMIC AWARENESS AND PHONICS

• **Listen for Initial and Final Sounds** Say a sound (e.g., /s/) and a word that begins or ends with the sound. Have students tell you whether they hear the sound at the beginning or at the end of the word. Some words to use are: *gas, map, ham, sit, net, ten.*

• **Blend Sounds to Decode Words** Distribute letter cards for *a, h, s, f, m,* and *t* (see pages T33–T38). Have students spell and blend *at,* then add a letter or change a letter to spell and blend *hat, sat, fat,* and *mat.*

BASIC VOCABULARY AND LANGUAGE DEVELOPMENT

OBJECTIVES

Function: Give Information

Concepts and Vocabulary:
❶ School Subjects; ❶ Telling Time

Patterns and Structures: ❶ *What time is it?;* ❶ *It is _____.; It is time for _____.*

Viewing: Interpret a Visual Image

TELL TIME

1 Introduce Clock Time Say: *It is now 8:45 a.m. and Carlos is getting ready to go to his classes. Soon we will meet some of his teachers, but first we'll practice telling time.* Turn to **Student Journal** page 20 and read the clocks. (Or just show various times on a clock and read them.) Explain that *a.m.* means "after midnight, but before 12 noon," and that *p.m.* means "after 12 noon, but before midnight." Ask volunteers to read different times you set on a clock.

2 Introduce the Patterns: *What time is it?* and *It is _____.* Model talking about time. Ask: *What time is it?* Point to a clock and use the pattern to answer: *It is 9:15 a.m.*

▶ **Student Journal** page 20

GIVE INFORMATION

3 Learn About Schedules Point to the Class Schedule and say: *The schedule shows Carlos when and where to go. It also tells the teacher for each class.* Read aloud the schedule and have students point to the matching photos.

4 Introduce the Pattern: *It is time for _____.* Relate the Class Schedule to the time. Point to the first line and say: *At 8:30 a.m., it is time for homeroom.* Have students give more information from the schedule.

CLOSE AND ASSESS

Call out a time: *It's 2:10 p.m.* and have the volunteers tell about their classes: *It's time for math.*

Time: 8:45 a.m.

Here are some teachers.

light switch

Numbers All...

2+2

transparency

overhead projector

dictionary

Dictionary

MS. CHANDANI, ESL TEACHER

uniform

mat

MR. DUNCAN, P.E. TEACHER

scale

MRS. SATO, SCIENCE TEACHER

10

REACHING ALL STUDENTS

Language Development
TELLING TIME

Play Clock Concentration Draw clock faces with different times on index cards. On separate cards write the corresponding times. Mix the cards and arrange them face down in several rows. Divide the class into two teams. Have a student from Team A turn over two cards. If the cards match, the player says the time and the team keeps the cards. Continue play until all cards have been matched. The team with the most matches wins.

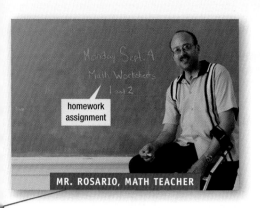

homework assignment

MR. ROSARIO, MATH TEACHER

Class Schedule

Class	Time	Room	Teacher
Homeroom	8:30 a.m.	113	Mrs. Terry
Math	8:45 a.m.	124	Mr. Rosario
ESL, Lang. Arts	9:45 a.m.	118	Ms. Chandani
ESL, Reading	10:45 a.m.	121	Mr. Motts
P.E.	11:45 a.m.	Gym	Mr. Duncan
Lunch	12:40 p.m.		
Science	1:10 p.m.	116	Mrs. Sato
Social Studies	2:10 p.m.	233	Mrs. Varela
Band practice	3:10 p.m.	Auditorium	Mrs. Cally

map

globe

MRS. VARELA, SOCIAL STUDIES TEACHER

Pronunciation of Names
Rosario   rō **sar** ē ō
Chandani   chahn **dahn** ē
Sato   **sah** tō
Varela   var **el** ah

Listen and Learn

Maylin: It is time for math class. Who is your math teacher?

Carlos: Mr. Rosario.

Maylin: He is a good teacher.

Carlos: Where is your ESL class?

Maylin: It's in Room 118.

Carlos: Who is your teacher?

Maylin: Ms. Chandani. She is really nice!

11

HOME CONNECTION

Class Schedule Have students take home a copy of their class schedules to show family members. Suggest that they draw a clock face to show the times of their classes. Provide frames for students to practice in school:

Math class is at 8:45 a.m.
It is in Room 124.
Mr. Rosario is my teacher.

BASIC VOCABULARY AND LANGUAGE DEVELOPMENT

OBJECTIVES

Functions: Listen Actively; Repeat Spoken Language; Ask and Answer Questions; Give Information

Patterns and Structures:

❶ *Where is* _____*?;* ❶ *Who is* _____*?;*
❶ *Here is* _____*.;* ❶ *Here are* _____*.*

ASK AND ANSWER QUESTIONS

1 Introduce the Patterns: *Where/Who is* _____*?* Play the "Listen and Learn" conversation on the **Lakeside Language Tape/CD.** Students follow along with the conversation, then listen to segments and echo lines. Finally, they chime in with Carlos.

Side A

CD Track 4

2 Talk About Schedules Have students write their class schedules on **Student Journal** page 21. Explain how to ask and answer questions:

- Use *Where is* to ask about a place: **Where is** *P.E. class?*
- Answer with *It's:* **It's** *in the gym.*
- Use *Who is* to ask about a person: **Who is** *the math teacher?*
- Answer with the teacher's name: **Mr. Rosario** *is the math teacher.*

▶ **Student Journal** page 21

GIVE INFORMATION

3 Introduce the Patterns: *Here is/are* _____*.* Arrange combinations of objects around the room. Hold up a book and explain: *Use* Here is *to tell about one thing: "Here is a book."* Next hold up three pencils and explain: *Use* Here are *to tell about more than one thing: "Here are three pencils."*

▶ **Student Journal** page 22

CLOSE AND ASSESS

Have partners move around the room and say sentences about different objects: *Here is a map. Here are four pens.*

LANGUAGE AND LITERACY: HIGH FREQUENCY WORDS

OBJECTIVES

Learning to Read:
❶ Recognize High Frequency Words

INTRODUCE

1 Learn New Words Place a word and its letter tiles on the screen as you work through the Strategy steps. For *your,* say:

1. *First, look at the word.* (Display the word tile for *your.*)

2. *Now listen to the word:* your, your.

3. *Listen to the word in a sentence:* Where is your science class?

4. *Say the word after me:* your.

5. *Spell the word:* y-o-u-r. (Say each letter as you place the tile. Point to each tile and have students spell the word.)

6. *Say the word again:* your.

Repeat the process for the other words, using these context sentences:

- **She** is in Room 121.
- **He** is Mr. Duncan.
- **Who are some good** teachers?
- Now it is **time** for class.

PRACTICE

2 Build Sentences Set out the word tiles at random and read aloud a sentence: *Who is she?* Place the tile for the first word to the left. Have students say which tiles to place next. Place the punctuation tile. Have students read the question. Continue with: *Who is he? Who are you? Where is your school?*

APPLY

3 Read New Words Have students find the new words on pages 10–11.

▶ **Student Journal** page 23

CLOSE AND ASSESS

Display the words one at a time for students to read.

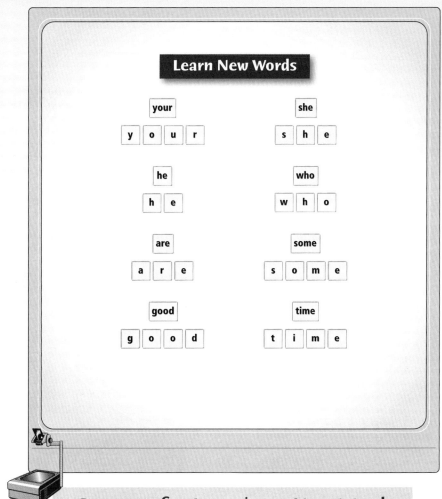

Strategy for Learning a New Word

1. Look at the word.
2. Listen to the word.
3. Listen to the word in a sentence.
4. Say the word.
5. Spell the word.
6. Say the word again.

REACHING ALL STUDENTS

Multimodal Practice
RECOGNIZE HIGH FREQUENCY WORDS

Distribute sets of cards with the words printed lightly in pencil. Also display the words on a chart. Then provide coaching for each activity:

Kinesthetic One group of students carefully outlines the shapes of the words on the cards and then erases the letters.

Visual Other students match the outline shapes with the words on display.

Auditory Then one student can reprint the words inside the shapes, pronounce each word correctly, and have the group echo it.

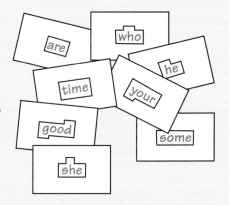

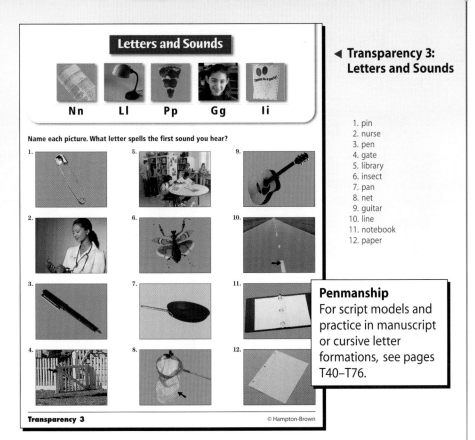

Letters and Sounds

Nn   Ll   Pp   Gg   Ii

Name each picture. What letter spells the first sound you hear?

◄ **Transparency 3:
Letters and Sounds**

1. pin
2. nurse
3. pen
4. gate
5. library
6. insect
7. pan
8. net
9. guitar
10. line
11. notebook
12. paper

Transparency 3   © Hampton-Brown

Penmanship
For script models and practice in manuscript or cursive letter formations, see pages T40–T76.

▼ **Script for Transparency 3**

Letters and Sounds

1. Develop Phonemic Awareness
Count Words in Sentences/Match Initial Sounds Say a sentence and have students count each word they hear: *Nora likes pink gum.* Then ask: *How many words are in this sentence?* (4) Repeat for: *Len eats pizza for lunch.* (5) Next, say: *Listen to these two words:* nurse, net. *Say the words with me:* nurse, net. *Do they begin with the same sound?* (yes) Repeat with these word pairs: *note, lamp; pin, pencil; gate, insect; line, library; girl, guitar; in, on; line, net; pan, nurse.*

2. Associate Letters and Sounds
Learn Consonant Names, Sounds, and Formations Point to the newspaper on **Transparency 3**. Say: *This is a newspaper. Say* newspaper *with me:* newspaper. Then point to *Nn* and say: *This is capital* N, *and this is lowercase* n. *The letter* n *spells the first sound you hear in* newspaper. The first sound is /n/. *Say* /nnn/ *with me:* /nnn/. Point to the *n* and ask: *What is the letter? What is its sound?* Trace the *Nn* on the transparency as you explain how to form the letters and have students "write" the letters in the air. Repeat for *l, p,* and *g.* Then explain: *The letters* n, l, p, *and* g *are **consonants**—they spell consonant sounds.*

Learn the Name, Sound, and Formation for the Vowel *Ii* Point to *Ii* and say: *This is the letter* i—*capital* I *and lowercase* i. *The letter* i *is a **vowel**.* Point to the invitation and say: *Say* invitation *with me:* invitation. *Say its first sound:* /iii/. *The sound* /iii/ *is a vowel sound. When you say a vowel sound, you keep your mouth open and let the air flow out. Try it:* /iii/. Then say: *The letter* i *spells the vowel sound* /i/ *you hear in* invitation. Point to the *i* and ask: *What is the letter? What is its sound?* Then teach students how to form capital and lowercase *i.*

Practice Have students number a paper from 1–12. For Item 1, say: *What is in this picture? Let's say the word and then its first sound:* pin, /p/. *What letter spells* /p/ *as in* pin? *That's right,* p. Point to the *Pp* on the transparency. Have students write a capital and lowercase *p* by Item 1 on their papers. Repeat for Items 2–12.

LANGUAGE AND LITERACY: PHONICS

OBJECTIVES
Learning to Read: Build Oral Vocabulary; Develop Phonemic Awareness; ❶ Associate Letters and Sounds

TEACH LETTERS AND SOUNDS

1 **Build Oral Vocabulary** Display Transparency 3. Play a game of "I Spy," giving clues until students find the picture. For example, for Item 9, say:

• *I spy a guitar. You play music with a guitar. It has strings and a long neck.*

When students find the guitar, say: *Yes, **this is a guitar** (point).* Repeat the game to build context for the other words.

2 **Develop Phonemic Awareness** Remove the transparency and work through Step 1 of the script.

3 **Associate Letters and Sounds** Display Transparency 3 again. Work through Step 2 of the script.

▶ **Student Journal** pages 24, 25

CLOSE AND ASSESS
Say the words *net, pencil, gate, line,* and *insect* one at a time. Have students write the letter that stands for the first sound in the word on a card and hold it up.

Review and Reteaching
PHONEMIC AWARENESS AND PHONICS

• **Match Initial Sounds** Say a sound and two words. Ask students to tell you which word begins with the sound you name. Some sounds and words to use are: /n/ *girl, net;* /l/ *lamp, pen;* /p/ *nurse, pizza;* /g/ *gate, line;* /i/ *insect, apple.*

• **Match Letters and Sounds** Set out classroom objects or pictures whose names begin with the sounds taught to date. Distribute corresponding letter cards (see pages T33–T38). Have students name each object, say its first sound, and attach the appropriate letter card.

BASIC VOCABULARY AND LANGUAGE DEVELOPMENT

OBJECTIVES

Concepts and Vocabulary:
🔵 Classroom Activities

Viewing: Interpret a Visual Image

USE WORDS FOR CLASSROOM ACTIVITIES

1 **Identify Actions** Direct attention to pages 12–13. Explain: *Now it is 9:10 a.m. Carlos is in math class. Let's look at some of the things he does in math class.* Look at the photos and read aloud the captions.

2 **Present Words for Classroom Activities** Post a chart of common classroom actions:

Classroom Activities

answer	find	sit
ask	listen	stand
carry	look	talk
close	open	type
cut	point to	use
draw	read	work
erase	sharpen	write

As you read aloud the list, act out each action and have students copy you and say the word.

3 **Pantomime** Have volunteers pantomime a classroom activity from the chart for other students to guess.

▶ **Student Journal** page 26

CLOSE AND ASSESS

Call on students to show and tell about two actions they do at school.

Time: 9:10 a.m.

Here is a math class.

I work at my desk.

I raise my hand.

I write a problem on the board.

problem

solution

I write the answer to the problem. I show my work.

I work with a group.

12

REACHING ALL STUDENTS

Vocabulary
CLASSROOM ACTIVITIES

Photo Captions Have small groups page through the text to find photographs of people doing classroom activities. Provide self-stick notes for students to create first-person captions for the individuals in the pictures. To model this activity, turn to pages 6–7 and write captions for the teacher: *I talk to the students. I stand in front of the board.* Affix the label near the teacher. Afterwards page through the book and ask the groups to share their captions.

I read my textbook.

I write my name on my worksheet.

I read my worksheet.
I write the answers.

Pronunciation of Name
Rosario rō **sar** ē ō

Listen and Learn

Mr. Rosario:	Which circle shows 25% of 4? Show me.
Carlos:	Here is the circle. It is Circle C.
Mr. Rosario:	Good. Point to the circle that shows 50% of 4.
Carlos:	Here is the circle. It is Circle A.
Mr. Rosario:	Good. Now show me the circle that shows 75% of 4.
Carlos:	Here is the circle. It is Circle D.
Mr. Rosario:	Good job, Carlos!

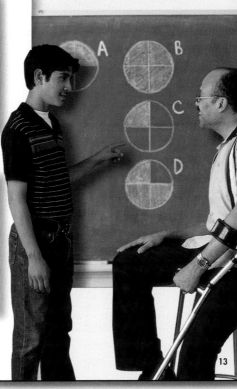

13

BASIC VOCABULARY AND LANGUAGE DEVELOPMENT

OBJECTIVES

Functions: Listen Actively; Repeat Spoken Language; Give and Carry Out Commands

Concepts and Vocabulary:
❶ Shapes; Commands

Patterns and Structures:
Show me _____.; Point to _____.

USE NAMES OF SHAPES

1 **Introduce Shapes** Draw a circle, a square, a triangle, and a rectangle. Trace the outline as you name and describe each shape: *A triangle has three sides.*

2 **Identify Shapes** Use chart paper to draw a large pattern that includes combinations of the four shapes. Give instructions for volunteers to follow: *Color a square red. Count the circles.*

GIVE AND CARRY OUT COMMANDS

3 **Introduce Commands** Explain: *When you give a command, you tell someone what to do.* Then play the "Listen and Learn" conversation on the **Lakeside Language Tape/CD**. It contains good modeling of commands and responses to commands.

Side A
CD
Track 5

4 **Introduce the Patterns:** *Point to _____.* **and** *Show me _____.* Post these sentence frames:

> Point to _____.
> Show me _____.

Use the patterns to give commands: *Point to Carlos's teacher. Show me a calculator.* Then have partners give and carry out commands.

▶ **Student Journal** pages 27, 28

CLOSE AND ASSESS

Write commands on several slips of paper; for example: *Point to Jan's desk. Show me a blue pen.* Volunteers can pick up a slip and carry out the command.

Language Development

GIVE AND CARRY OUT COMMANDS

Divide the class into four teams and assign one shape—circle, triangle, rectangle, or square—to each team. Have each team locate all items in the classroom that have their assigned shape. Students from each group can give commands for a student in another group to follow: *Point to a circle. Show me a square.* Give each group the opportunity to give and carry out commands.

LANGUAGE AND LITERACY: HIGH FREQUENCY WORDS

Learning to Read:
❶ Recognize High Frequency Words

INTRODUCE

1 Learn New Words Place a word and its letter tiles on the screen as you work through the Strategy steps. For example, for *work,* say:

1. *First, look at the word.* (Display the word tile for *work.*)

2. *Now listen to the word:* work, work.

3. *Listen to the word in a sentence:* I work at my desk.

4. *Say the word after me:* work.

5. *Spell the word:* w-o-r-k. (As you say each letter, place the corresponding letter tile. Point to each tile and have students spell the word.)

6. *Say the word again:* work.

Repeat the process for the other words, using these context sentences:

• I **read** a problem.
• I work **with** my teacher.
• I **write** an **answer**.
• I **point to** my worksheet.

PRACTICE

2 Build Sentences Say each word as you place its tile on the screen: *Point to the ____. Here is the ____. Here are the ____.* Model reading the text and filling in the blanks: *Point to the worksheet. Here is the worksheet. Here are the pencils.* Have one partner give the command and the other respond.

APPLY

3 Read New Words Have students find the new words on pages 12–13.

▶ **Student Journal** page 29

CLOSE AND ASSESS

Display the words one at a time for students to read.

Learn New Words

work	read
with	write
answer	point
to	

Strategy for Learning a New Word

1. Look at the word.
2. Listen to the word.
3. Listen to the word in a sentence.
4. Say the word.
5. Spell the word.
6. Say the word again.

REACHING ALL STUDENTS

Reading Fluency
RECOGNIZE HIGH FREQUENCY WORDS

To build automaticity with the new high frequency words:

• Display the word tiles on the overhead, one at a time. Scramble the letter tiles for the word below it. (Add distractor letters, for more of a challenge). Have volunteers rearrange the letter tiles and read the word.

• Use letter tiles on the overhead to spell out words from the list. Pause after each letter to see if students can identify the word you are spelling. After a word is identified, ask a volunteer to complete it.

Blend Words with Short i

Blend the sounds to read each word.

it	in	an
sit	pin	man
hit	pig	fan

Read each word. Which picture goes with the word?

1. pig
2. man
3. pin
4. fan

A.   B.   C.   D.

Transparency 4   © Hampton-Brown

◀ **Transparency 4: Blending**

Penmanship
For script models and practice in writing words in manuscript or cursive with correct letter spacing, see pages T40–T76.

Materials
Letter tiles for:

a	f	g	h	i
m	n	p	s	t

▼ **Script for Transparency 4**

Blend Words with Short *i*

1. Develop Phonemic Awareness
Match Initial Sounds/Match Final Sounds Say: *Listen to these two words:* it, in. *Say the words with me:* it, in. *The first sound in these words is the same:* /iii/. *Now listen to these two words:* it, at. *Say the words with me:* it, at. *Is the first sound in each word the same?* (no) Continue with word pairs *sit, lid; if, is; pig, hit; gift, girl.* Then say: *Now listen to these two words:* pin, man. *Say the words with me:* pin, man. *They end with the same sound:* /n/. *Here are two more words:* pig, in. *Say the words with me:* pig, in. *Is the last sound in each word the same?* (no) Continue with word pairs *lip, pit; sit, hat; pan, fin; big, fig; if, in.*

2. Blend Sounds to Read Words
Model Set letter tile *i* at the left in the box on **Transparency 4** and letter tile *t* at the right. Point to *i* and say: *The sound for this letter is* /iii/. As you say the sound, slide *i* next to *t,* and then put your finger under *t.* Say: *I can blend the sound* /iii/ *with the sound of the letter* t: /iiit/. *Now I'm going to say the word fast:* it. Summarize: *You can blend sounds like this to read a word. Just say the sound for the first letter, and blend it into the sound for the next letter.* Demonstrate again: Point to *i* and say: *Say the sound for* i *with me:* /iii/. *Repeat for* t: /t/. Then slide a finger below the letters *it* and say: *Help me blend the two sounds:* /iiit/. *Now let's say the word:* it. Then leave *it* at the right in the box, add letter tile *s* at the left, and repeat the process to read *sit.* Remove the *s* and repeat the process to read *hit.*

Practice Have students read the words *it, sit,* and *hit* below the box. Then repeat Model and Practice for the other two word sets.

3. Match Words and Pictures
Point to Item 1. Say: *Let's read this word.* Slide a finger slowly under the letters to lead students in sounding out the word: /piiig/, *pig.* Then say: *Now let's look at the pictures. Which of these pictures—A, B, C, or D—shows a pig?* (D) Repeat the process for Items 2, 3, and 4.

LANGUAGE AND LITERACY: PHONICS

OBJECTIVES
Learning to Read: Build Oral Vocabulary; Develop Phonemic Awareness; Blend Sounds to Decode Words

TEACH BLENDING

1 Build Oral Vocabulary Display Transparency 4. Use *it, sit,* and *hit* in sentences to build meaning.

- *I **sit** in a chair* (pantomime). ***It** is big. Can you **hit** a ball?* (pantomime)

Use the pictures to develop the meaning of the words *pin, fan, man,* and *pig.* For example:

- *This is a **fan**. When a **fan** is on, it spins and blows air. It makes us feel cool.*

2 Develop Phonemic Awareness Remove the transparency and work through Step 1 of the script.

3 Blend Sounds to Read Words Display Transparency 4 again. Work through Steps 2 and 3 of the script.

▶ **Student Journal** pages 30, 31

CLOSE AND ASSESS
Display *hit, pin, sit, fan,* and *pig.* Have students identify the sounds in each word and blend them to read the word.

Review and Reteaching
PHONEMIC AWARENESS AND PHONICS

- **Listen for Initial and Final Sounds** Say a sound (e.g., /p/) and a word that begins or ends with the sound. Have students tell you whether they hear the sound at the beginning or at the end of the word. Some words to use are: *pin, map, lamp, pill, big, get, pen, note.*

- **Blend Sounds to Decode Words** Distribute letter cards for *i, t, h, s, p, a,* and *f* (see pages T33–T38). Have students spell and blend *it,* then add a letter or change a letter to spell and blend *hit, sit, pit, fit, fat,* and *pat.*

BASIC VOCABULARY AND LANGUAGE DEVELOPMENT

USE NAMES OF SCHOOL OBJECTS AND PERSONNEL

1 **Introduce School Objects and Personnel** Explain: *It's now 9:40 a.m. Carlos goes to the main office.* Point to the school workers and explain their jobs; for example: *The principal is in charge of the school.* Then point out the objects and explain how each object is used.

GIVE PERSONAL INFORMATION

2 **Introduce the Pattern:** *My name is* ———. Explain that students can introduce themselves by saying: *Hi. My name is* ———. Have partners practice introducing themselves.

3 **Introduce the Pattern:** *My phone number is* ———. Explain: *To call someone on the telephone, you need the phone number.* Write the school number and say: *At work, my phone number is 555-2467. To tell someone your phone number, you can say: "My phone number is* ———.*"*

▶ **Student Journal** page 32

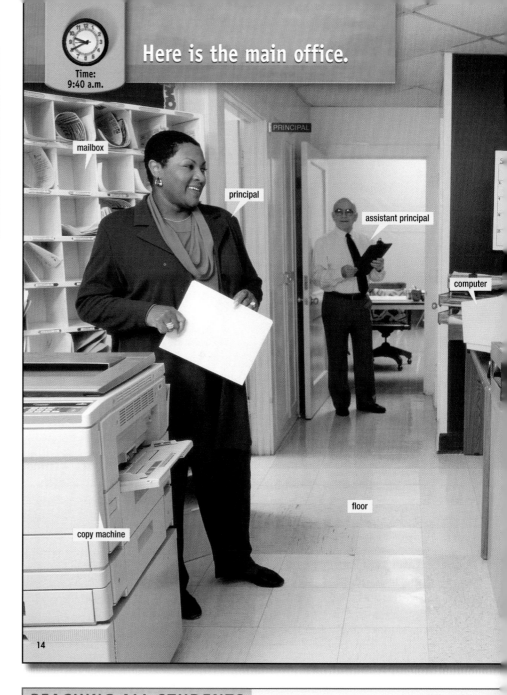

Time: 9:40 a.m.

Here is the main office.

mailbox

principal

assistant principal

computer

floor

copy machine

14

REACHING ALL STUDENTS

COMMUNITY CONNECTION

Community Service Numbers
Provide telephone books and brochures, or use local government Internet Web sites. Have groups find information for community services, such as the fire department, the police station, libraries, hospitals, and community centers. Groups can add the information to a class telephone directory. Make copies for students to use at home.

ceiling

bulletin board

calendar

secretary

telephone

Pronunciation of Name
Cruz   krüz

Listen and Learn

Carlos: Hi, Mrs. Cruz, my name
is Carlos Parra.
Where is the telephone?
I need to call my mom.

Mrs. Cruz: What is her phone
number?

Carlos: 555-3298.

Mrs. Cruz: Is this a work
number?

Carlos: Yes. My mom is
at work. She is a
secretary, like you.

15

Language Development

ASK FOR INFORMATION

Invite pairs of volunteers to role-play a
talk show interview, with one student
as the host and another as the guest.
The class can represent the audience.
The host asks questions with *what* and
*where: What is your name? Where is your
home?* The guest can answer with
personal information, or take the role of
a fictional character or famous person.
Later, have the audience pose questions
for the guest to answer.

BASIC VOCABULARY AND LANGUAGE DEVELOPMENT

OBJECTIVES

Functions: Listen Actively; Repeat Spoken
Language; Ask for Information; Express
Needs

Patterns and Structures:
❶ *Where is* _____?; ❶ *What is* _____?;
❶ *I need to* _____.

ASK FOR INFORMATION

1 **Introduce the Patterns:**
***Where/What is* _____?**
Play the "Listen and Learn"
conversation on the **Lakeside
Language Tape/CD**. Students will
listen twice to the conversation, then
echo lines and chime in with Carlos.

Side A

CD Track 6

2 **Ask and Answer Questions** Turn to
Student Journal page 33 and explain:
*When a question asks "What is," the
answer tells about a thing. When the
question asks "Where is," the answer
tells about a place.*

▶ **Student Journal** page 33

EXPRESS NEEDS

3 **Introduce the Pattern:** *I need to*
_____. Post sentence pairs to model
completing the pattern with a verb:

> My pencil is dull. I need to <u>sharpen</u> it.
> The class is starting. I need to <u>sit</u>.

Give scenarios and have students
create sentences with the pattern.

• I am tired. (I need to rest.)
• I have a test. (I need to study.)

4 **Use the Pattern:** *I need to* _____.
Have partners find pictures of people
in various settings. Help them add
speech balloons that express each
person's needs.

▶ **Student Journal** page 34

CLOSE AND ASSESS

Partners can role-play a school worker on
pages 14–15. Have them ask a question
or express a need.

LANGUAGE AND LITERACY: HIGH FREQUENCY WORDS

OBJECTIVES

Learning to Read:
❶ Recognize High Frequency Words

INTRODUCE

1 Learn New Words Place a word and its letter tiles on the screen as you work through the Strategy steps. For example, for *what*, say:

1. *First, look at the word.* (Display the word tile for *what*.)

2. *Now listen to the word:* what, what.

3. *Listen to the word in a sentence:* What is your name?

4. *Say the word after me:* what.

5. *Spell the word:* w-h-a-t. (As you say each letter, place the corresponding letter tile. Point to each tile and have students spell the word.)

6. *Say the word again:* what.

Repeat the process for the other words, using these context sentences. Point out the new meaning for the word *to:*

• My **name** is Maylin.
• I **need to** work with Carlos.
• I will **call** Carlos.
• The phone **number** is 555-9907.

PRACTICE

2 Sort Words Place the word tiles on the screen in a random arrangement. Have students sort the words to make this group: words that start with *n*.

APPLY

3 Read New Words Have students find the new words on pages 14–15.

▶ **Student Journal** page 35

CLOSE AND ASSESS

Display the words one at a time for students to read.

Learn New Words

what	name
w h a t	n a m e
need	to
n e e d	t o
call	number
c a l l	n u m b e r

Strategy for Learning a New Word

1. Look at the word.
2. Listen to the word.
3. Listen to the word in a sentence.
4. Say the word.
5. Spell the word.
6. Say the word again.

REACHING ALL STUDENTS

Reading Fluency
RECOGNIZE HIGH FREQUENCY WORDS

To build automaticity with the new high frequency words:

• Provide copies of an emergency procedures page from a telephone directory or other source. Have small groups look for the new words on it, and highlight the ones they find.

• Go over the procedure for reporting an emergency. Write the steps. Write over the new high frequency words in another color. Read the sentences aloud and pause at each new word for students to supply it.

1. Call the emergency number: 911.
2. Tell the person your name.
3. Tell what is wrong.
4. Say the address. You need to give the town, too.
5. Give the phone number.

IMPORTANT: Verify that 911 is the emergency number for your area. This can vary.

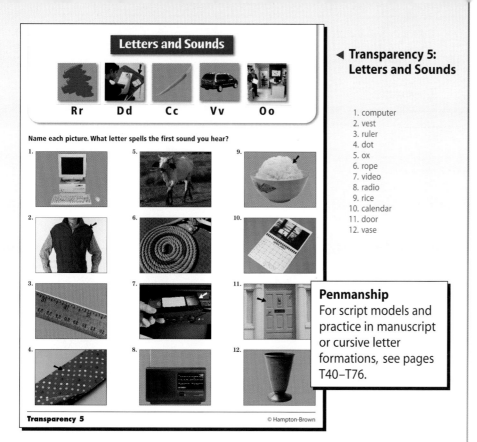

◄ Transparency 5: Letters and Sounds

1. computer
2. vest
3. ruler
4. dot
5. ox
6. rope
7. video
8. radio
9. rice
10. calendar
11. door
12. vase

Penmanship
For script models and practice in manuscript or cursive letter formations, see pages T40–T76.

▼ Script for Transparency 5

Letters and Sounds

1. Develop Phonemic Awareness

Count Words in Sentences/Match Initial Sounds Say a sentence and have students count each word they hear: *Who drives the red van?* Then ask: *How many words are in the sentence?* (5) Repeat for: *Who drives the red van down the street?* (8) Next, say: *Listen to these two words:* red, run. *Say the words with me:* red, run. *Do they begin with the same sound?* (yes) Repeat with these word pairs: *dot, door; cup, vest; rope, ruler; ox, on; van, vine; computer, calendar.*

2. Associate Letters and Sounds

Learn Consonant Names, Sounds, and Formations Point to the swatch of red on **Transparency 5**. Say: *This is the color red. Say* red *with me:* red. Then point to *Rr* and say: *This is capital* R, *and this is lowercase* r. *The letter* r *spells the first sound you hear in* red. *The first sound is* /r/. *Say* /rrr/ *with me:* /rrr/. Point to the *r* and ask: *What is the letter? What is its sound?* Trace the *Rr* on the transparency as you explain how to form the letters and have students "write" the letters in the air. Repeat the process for *d, c,* and *v.* Then explain: *The letters* r, d, c, *and* v *are called* ***consonants***—*they spell consonant sounds.*

Learn the Name, Sound, and Formation for the Vowel Oo Point to *Oo* and say: *This is the letter* o—*capital* O *and lowercase* o. *The letter* o *is a* ***vowel***. Point to the office and say: *Say* office *with me:* office. *Say its first sound:* /ooo/. *The sound* /ooo/ *is a vowel sound. When you say a vowel sound, you keep your mouth open and let the air flow out. Try it:* /ooo/. Then say: *The letter* o *spells the vowel sound* /o/ *you hear in* office. Point to the *o* and ask: *What is the letter? What is its sound?* Then teach students how to form capital and lowercase *o.*

Practice Have students number a paper from 1–12. For Item 1, say: *What is in this picture? Let's say the word and then its first sound:* computer, /k/. *What letter spells* /k/ *as in* computer? *That's right,* c. Point to the *Cc* on the transparency. Have students write a capital and lowercase *c* by Item 1 on their papers. Repeat the process for Items 2–12.

LANGUAGE AND LITERACY: PHONICS

OBJECTIVES

Learning to Read: Build Oral Vocabulary; Develop Phonemic Awareness; ❶ Associate Letters and Sounds

TEACH LETTERS AND SOUNDS

1 Build Oral Vocabulary Display Transparency 5. Play "I Spy," giving clues until students find the picture. For example, for Item 8, say:

• *I spy a radio. You can listen to music or the news on a radio. Some radios are small. You can carry them with you.*

When students find the radio, say: *Yes,* ***this is a radio*** (point). Repeat the game to build context for the other words.

2 Develop Phonemic Awareness Remove the transparency and work through Step 1 of the script.

3 Associate Letters and Sounds Display Transparency 5 again. Work through Step 2 of the script.

▶ **Student Journal** pages 36, 37

CLOSE AND ASSESS

Say the words *carrot, ox, rope, desk,* and *video* one at a time. Have the group write the letter that stands for the first sound in the word on a card and hold it up.

Review and Reteaching
PHONEMIC AWARENESS AND PHONICS

• **Isolate Sounds** Say words that begin with the sounds taught to date and ask students to tell you the first sound they hear in the word.

• **Match Letters and Sounds** Display transparencies for the letters and sounds taught to date. Have students name each picture at the top, say the first sound, and tell the name of the letter. Then distribute letter cards (see pages T33–T38). Say words that begin with the sounds taught to date, and have students hold up the letter that spells the first sound in the word.

BASIC VOCABULARY AND LANGUAGE DEVELOPMENT

OBJECTIVES

Function: Ask for and Give Information

Concepts and Vocabulary:
❶ Library Objects

Patterns and Structures: *What is in the _____?; A _____ is in the _____.; Some _____ are in the _____.; Plurals with -s*

Viewing: Interpret a Visual Image

USE NAMES OF LIBRARY OBJECTS

1 Introduce Library Objects Say: *At 11:00 a.m., Carlos goes to the school library. A library has books, magazines, and computers. A librarian helps you find books and materials.* Go over the labeled objects and show examples from your classroom.

ASK FOR AND GIVE INFORMATION

2 Introduce Plurals with -s Explain: *We add -s to show that there is more than one object.* Have students review the library scene and make a chart:

What is in the Library?

one	more than one
a globe	**two** chair**s**
a table	**two** door**s**

3 Introduce the Patterns: *What is in the _____?; A _____ is in the _____.; Some _____ are in the _____.*
Explain: *We use the question to ask what objects are in a place. We use the word* some *when we don't know how many objects there are or if the number is not important.*

4 Visit the School Library Ask the librarian to give a brief tour. Have students identify library objects.

▶ **Student Journal** page 38

CLOSE AND ASSESS

Assign groups different areas of the school. Have each group complete a chart headed "What is in the _____?" by listing items that are found in that place.

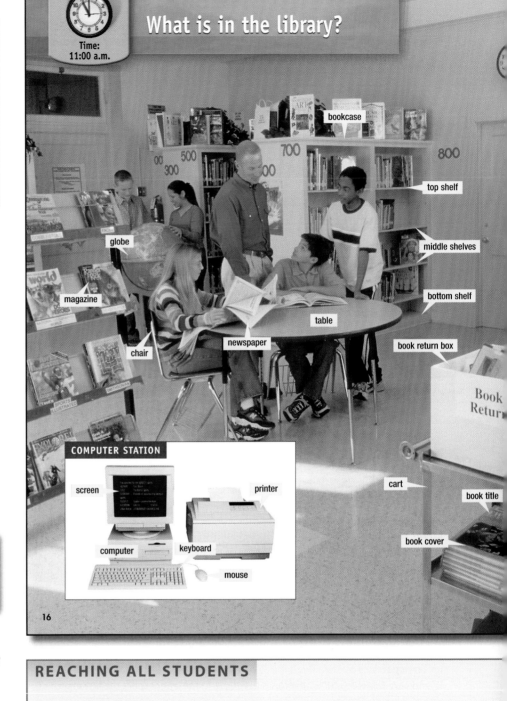

What is in the library?

Time: 11:00 a.m.

bookcase · top shelf · middle shelves · bottom shelf · globe · magazine · chair · newspaper · table · book return box · cart · book title · book cover

COMPUTER STATION

screen · printer · computer · keyboard · mouse

16

REACHING ALL STUDENTS

Vocabulary
LIBRARY OBJECTS

Library Tour Maps Have small groups make and label a drawing of the school library. Have groups compare drawings and make sure they have included all library objects. Then have group members take turns using the drawing to give a "tour" of the library. Encourage students to ask and answer questions about the library during the "tour."

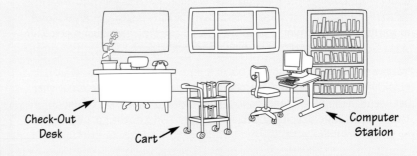

Check-Out Desk · Cart · Computer Station

Listen and Learn

Carlos:	Will you help me find a book, Mrs. Jones?
Mrs. Jones:	Sure. Do you like sports?
Carlos:	Yes. I like sports a lot!
Mrs. Jones:	Here is a good book for you. The title is *The Best in Sports*.
Carlos:	Does the book show a picture of soccer?
Mrs. Jones:	Yes, it does. You will like the book!

lamp

librarian

check-out desk

encyclopedias

17

Multimodal Practice
QUESTIONS AND ANSWERS

Visual Have students copy the first three lines of the conversation onto sentence strips, and then cut them apart to create word and end-mark cards.

Kinesthetic Students study the printed conversation and then use the cards to rebuild the lines.

Auditory Students can read the reconstructed conversation aloud for the group.

BASIC VOCABULARY AND LANGUAGE DEVELOPMENT

OBJECTIVES

Functions: Listen Actively; Repeat Spoken Language; Express Likes; Ask and Answer Questions

Patterns and Structures: *Will you _____?;* ❶ *Does _____?; Do you like _____?;* ❶ *I like _____.*

EXPRESS LIKES

1 Introduce the Patterns: *Do you like _____? and I like _____.* Play the "Listen and Learn" conversation on the **Lakeside Language Tape/CD**. Students will listen to the conversation, then echo one line at a time, and chime in on Carlos's part.

Side B · CD Track 7

2 People Hunt Post sentence frames:

> I like _____.
> Do you like _____?

Have students draw something they like, such as a sport, a food, or a hobby. Then have students mingle and ask other students if they like the same thing: *I like books. Do you like books?* Students who answer "yes" can sign the picture.

▶ **Student Journal** page 39

ASK AND ANSWER QUESTIONS

3 Introduce the Patterns: *Will you _____? and Does _____?* Review the conversation and explain: *You can start questions with* Will you *or* Does.

Set out several books and pose questions: *Will you help me find a book about sports? Does it tell about baseball?* Students can answer, then ask new questions.

▶ **Student Journal** page 40

CLOSE AND ASSESS

Display the four language patterns presented and have partners role-play a conversation between a student and a librarian.

LANGUAGE AND LITERACY: HIGH FREQUENCY WORDS

OBJECTIVES

Learning to Read:
❶ Recognize High Frequency Words

INTRODUCE

1 Learn New Words Place a word and its letter tiles on the screen as you work through the Strategy steps. For *for,* say:

1. *First, look at the word.* (Display the word tile for *for.*)

2. *Now listen to the word:* for, for.

3. *Listen to the word in a sentence:* I have a book for you.

4. *Say the word after me:* for.

5. *Spell the word:* f-o-r. (Say each letter as you place the tile. Point to each tile and have students spell the word.)

6. *Say the word again:* for.

Repeat the process for the other words, using these context sentences:

- Look **in** the library.
- **Does** it have a good book for **me**?
- I **will help** you.
- **Do** you **like** the **picture**?

PRACTICE

2 Build Sentences Set out the word tiles at random and read aloud a question: *Do you like this picture?* Place the tile for the first word to the left. Then have students tell you which tiles to place next. Place the punctuation tile. Have students read the question in unison. Continue with: *Does he help you? Does she see it?*

APPLY

3 Read New Words Have students find the new words on pages 16–17.

▶ **Student Journal** page 41

CLOSE AND ASSESS

Display the words one at a time for students to read.

Learn New Words

Strategy for Learning a New Word

1. Look at the word.
2. Listen to the word.
3. Listen to the word in a sentence.
4. Say the word.
5. Spell the word.
6. Say the word again.

REACHING ALL STUDENTS

Reading Fluency
RECOGNIZE HIGH FREQUENCY WORDS

To build automaticity with the new high frequency words:

- Display the word list. Give two clues for each word—the number of letters in it, and the letter it starts with—and have students guess it. Say: *Which word has two letters and starts with* d? (*do*) If students guess an incorrect word, go over why it doesn't work: *The word* does *starts with* d, *but it has more than two letters, doesn't it?*

- Give small groups the letter tiles for three of the words. Have them unscramble the letters to "find" their words. Groups can take turns leading the class in reading their words.

Blend Words with Short o

Blend the sounds to read each word.

on	not	hot
an	dot	hat
in	pot	hit

Read each word. Which picture goes with the word?

1. mop
2. cap
3. pot
4. map

A.   B.   C.   D.

© Hampton-Brown

◀ **Transparency 6: Blending**

Penmanship
For script models and practice in writing words in manuscript or cursive with correct letter spacing, see pages T40–T76.

Materials
Letter tiles for:

a	d	h	i
n	o	p	t

▼ **Script for Transparency 6**

Blend Words with Short o

1. Develop Phonemic Awareness
Match Initial Sounds/Match Final Sounds Say: *Listen to these two words:* on, ox. *Say the words with me:* on, ox. *The first sound in these words is the same: /ooo/. Now listen to these two words:* on, it. *Say the words with me:* on, it. *Is the first sound in each word the same?* (no) Continue with word pairs *ask, an; on, pot; top, not; hot, hit; in, if.* Then say: *Now listen to these two words:* hop, map. *Say the words with me:* hop, map. *They end with the same sound: /p/. Here are two more words:* ham, hot. *Say the words with me:* ham, hot. *Is the last sound in each word the same?* (no) Continue with word pairs *dot, run; rod, lid; van, on; mop, cap.*

2. Blend Sounds to Read Words
Model Set letter tile *o* at the left in the box on **Transparency 6** and letter tile *n* at the right. Point to *o* and say: *The sound for this letter is /ooo/. As you say the sound, slide* o *next to* n, *and then put your finger under* n. Say: *I can blend the sound /ooo/ with the sound of the letter* n: /ooonnn/. *Now I'm going to say the word fast:* on. Summarize: *You can blend sounds like this to read a word. Just say the sound for the first letter, and blend it into the sound for the next letter.* Demonstrate again: Point to *o* and say: *Say the sound for* o *with me: /ooo/.* Repeat for *n: /nnn/.* Then slide a finger below the letters *on* and say: *Help me blend the two sounds: /ooonnn/. Now let's say the word:* on. Then remove *o* and leave *n* at the right in the box. Add letter tile *a* at the left, and repeat the process to read *an.* Replace the *a* with *i* and repeat the process to read *in.*

Practice Have students read the words *on, an,* and *in* below the box. Then repeat Model and Practice for the other two word sets.

3. Match Words and Pictures
Point to Item 1. Say: *Let's read this word.* Slide a finger slowly under the letters to lead students in sounding out the word: /mmmooop/, *mop.* Then say: *Now let's look at the pictures. Which of these pictures—A, B, C, or D—shows a mop?* (A) Repeat the process for Items 2, 3, and 4.

LANGUAGE AND LITERACY: PHONICS

OBJECTIVES
Learning to Read: Build Oral Vocabulary; Develop Phonemic Awareness; Blend Sounds to Decode Words

TEACH BLENDING

1 Build Oral Vocabulary Display Transparency 6. Use *on, dot,* and *hot* in sentences to build meaning:

- *I put my hand **on** the book* (pantomime). *A **dot** is a small circle with the color filled in* (demonstrate). *When it is **hot**, I like to swim.*

Use the pictures to develop the meaning of *mop, map, cap,* and *pot*:

- *This is a **mop**. You use a **mop** to clean a floor. You push the **mop**.*

2 Develop Phonemic Awareness Remove the transparency and work through Step 1 of the script.

3 Blend Sounds to Read Words Display Transparency 6 again. Work through Steps 2 and 3 of the script.

▶ **Student Journal** pages 42, 43

CLOSE AND ASSESS

Display *pot, map, hot, mop,* and *hit.* Have students identify the sounds in each word and blend them to read the word.

Review and Reteaching
PHONEMIC AWARENESS AND PHONICS

- **Create Rhyming Words** Arrange students in a circle. Choose a word from Transparencies 1–6, for example: *vest.* The two students to your right must agree on a word that rhymes with yours. Go around the circle, encouraging partners to add more rhyming words.

- **Blend Sounds to Decode Words** Distribute letter cards for *h, o, t, g, n, d, p, i,* and *a* (see pages T33–T38). Have students spell and blend *hot,* then change a letter to spell and blend *got, not, dot, pot, pit,* and *pat.*

BASIC VOCABULARY AND LANGUAGE DEVELOPMENT

OBJECTIVES

Functions: Listen Actively; Repeat Spoken Language; Express Likes

Concepts and Vocabulary: ❶ Sports

Patterns and Structures: ❶ *I like _____.*

Viewing: Interpret a Visual Image

USE SPORTS WORDS

1 Introduce Sports Words Explain: *It is now 12:00 p.m., or noon. Carlos is in P.E. class. "P.E." stands for physical education. Here, students play sports and exercise.* Use the photos to introduce sports words. Have students point to various objects as you say sentences: *Show me a softball glove.*

2 Visit the School Gym Ask a P.E. teacher to show sports equipment and demonstrate its use.

EXPRESS LIKES

3 Review the Pattern:
I like _____. Play the "Listen and Learn" conversation on the **Lakeside Language Tape/CD**. Students will listen once to the conversation, and then listen again, clapping each time they hear the word *like* or *likes*. Then they'll echo the lines, and finally chime in on Carlos's part.

Side B

CD Track 8

▶ **Student Journal** page 44

CLOSE AND ASSESS

Have volunteers pantomime sports they like for the class to guess. The student doing the pantomime confirms correct guesses: *Yes, I like tennis.*

Time: 12:00 p.m.

What do you do in P.E.?

basket

basketball

court

A GYM LOCKER

lock

sneakers

You can play basketball.

helmet

bat

mask

softball

umpire

glove

You can play softball.

18

REACHING ALL STUDENTS

HOME CONNECTION

Sports Booklets Model how to create a booklet by folding two sheets of paper in half and stapling them together at the center. Have students add the title: *We Like Sports.* On each of the four inner pages, have students copy the sentence frame: *I like _____.* Students can complete the first page with a favorite sport: *I like judo.* Encourage them to draw or use pictures from magazines and newspapers, writing labels for the people and equipment.

Then have students interview three family members about their favorite sports. The family can work together to create a new page for each sport. Have the family members sign their names and complete the sentence with the name of the sport. In class, students can decorate the cover of their booklet to reflect the contents.

We Like Sports

by the Cheng Family

You can run around the track.

You can play volleyball.

You can play soccer.

19

Listen and Learn

Dan: What sports do you like?

Carlos: I like soccer.

Dan: My friend Ron likes soccer, too. We also play basketball. Can you play basketball?

Carlos: Yes, I can play basketball. I like lots of sports.

Language Development
ASK AND ANSWER QUESTIONS

In small groups, have students show the drawings and sentences they made on **Student Journal** page 44. Encourage them to hold discussions. Provide frames:

> Do you like _____?
> I like _____.
>
> Can you _____?
> I can _____.

Students may record their discussions and play them for the class.

BASIC VOCABULARY AND LANGUAGE DEVELOPMENT

OBJECTIVES

Functions: Listen Actively; Ask and Answer Questions

Patterns and Structures:

❶ *Can you* _____?;

❶ *I can* _____.; ❶ *You can* _____.

ASK AND ANSWER QUESTIONS

1 Introduce the Pattern: *You can* _____. Read the captions on pages 18–19 and have students follow along. Then have students use the pattern to tell about a sport at your school: *At Lakeside, you can play volleyball.*

2 Introduce the Patterns: *Can you* _____*?* and *I can* _____. Post sentence frames:

> Can you _____?
> I can _____.

Then reread the caption for the bottom photo on page 18 and model adapting the text to form a new question and answer: *Can you play softball? I can play softball.* Use the scene for more ideas: *Can you hit the ball? Can you catch the ball?* Have partners work together to form more questions and answers.

3 Talk About Sports Turn to **Student Journal** page 45 and help students complete the sentences in Items 1–4 using the pattern *You can* _____. For the second activity, have partners complete questions with the pattern *Can you* _____*?*, then trade books to fill in the answers.

▶ **Student Journal** page 45

CLOSE AND ASSESS

Have partners use the patterns to ask and answer questions about sports or other activities.

Language Development **T19**

LANGUAGE AND LITERACY: HIGH FREQUENCY WORDS

OBJECTIVES

Learning to Read:
❶ Recognize High Frequency Words

INTRODUCE

1 Learn New Words Place a word and its letter tiles on the screen as you work through the Strategy steps. For example, for *play*, say:

1. *First, look at the word.* (Display the word tile for *play*.)

2. *Now listen to the word:* play, play.

3. *Listen to the word in a sentence:* Do you play soccer?

4. *Say the word after me:* play.

5. *Spell the word:* p-l-a-y. (As you say each letter, place the corresponding letter tile. Point to each tile and have students spell the word.)

6. *Say the word again:* play.

Repeat the process for the other words, using these context sentences:

• Where **can we** run?
• We can run **around** the track.
• We can play soccer, **too**.

PRACTICE

2 Build Sentences Say each word as you place its tile on the screen: *Can you play _____? No. I play _____.*

Model reading the text and filling in the blanks with the names of sports: *Can you play basketball? No. I play soccer.* Then one partner asks the question; the other answers.

APPLY

3 Read New Words Have students find the new words on pages 18–19.

▶ **Student Journal** page 46

CLOSE AND ASSESS

Display the words one at a time for students to read.

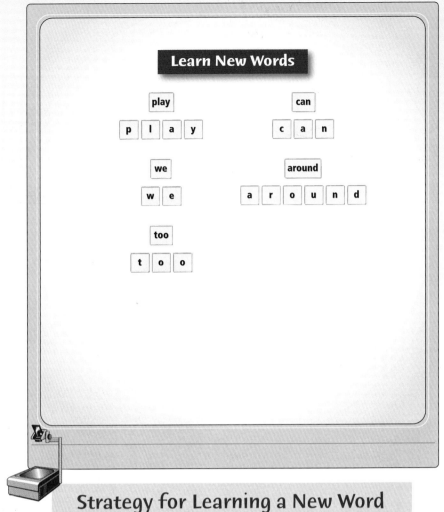

Strategy for Learning a New Word

1. Look at the word.
2. Listen to the word.
3. Listen to the word in a sentence.
4. Say the word.
5. Spell the word.
6. Say the word again.

REACHING ALL STUDENTS

Multimodal Practice
RECOGNIZE HIGH FREQUENCY WORDS

Display the sentences from Step 2. Then do the following activities.

Kinesthetic Students copy the sentences onto strips and cut them apart to make word and punctuation cards.

Visual Students reassemble the sentences to match those displayed.

Auditory Partners practice saying the sentences (filling in the blanks with sports), and then perform or tape their final reading.

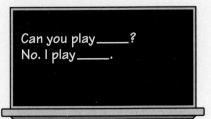

Letters and Sounds

| Jj | Bb | Ww | Kk | Ee |

Name each picture. What letter spells the first sound you hear?

1.
2.
3.
4.
5.
6.
7.
8.
9.
10.
11.
12.

◀ **Transparency 7: Letters and Sounds**

1. bench
2. keyboard
3. watch
4. jog
5. envelope
6. ball
7. jar
8. wallet
9. elbow
10. bat
11. kitchen
12. encyclopedia

Penmanship
For script models and practice in manuscript or cursive letter formations, see pages T40–T76.

Transparency 7   © Hampton-Brown

▼ **Script for Transparency 7**

Letters and Sounds

1. Develop Phonemic Awareness
Match Initial Sounds Say: *Listen to these two words:* jog, jar. *Say the words with me:* jog, jar. *Do they begin with the same sound?* (yes) Repeat with these word pairs: *jacket, kitchen; book, bench; key, kitchen; egg, ant; watch, window; envelope, egg; ball, basket; book, jog.*

2. Associate Letters and Sounds
Learn Consonant Names, Sounds, and Formations Point to the jacket on **Transparency 7**. Say: *This is a jacket. You can wear a jacket to keep warm. Say* jacket *with me:* jacket. Then point to *Jj* and say: *This is capital J, and this is lowercase j. The letter* j *spells the first sound you hear in* jacket. *The first sound is* /j/. *Say* /j/ *with me:* /j/. Point to the *j* and ask: *What is the letter? What is its sound?* Trace the *Jj* on the transparency as you explain how to form the letters and have students "write" the letters in the air. Repeat the process for *b, w,* and *k.* Point out that the letter *k* makes the same sound as the letter *c:* /k/. Then explain: *The letters* j, b, w, *and* k, *are called* **consonants**—*they spell consonant sounds.*

Learn the Name, Sound, and Formation for the Vowel *Ee* Point to *Ee* and say: *This is the letter* e—*capital* E *and lowercase* e. *The letter* e *is a* **vowel**. Point to the egg and say: *Say* egg *with me:* egg. *Say its first sound:* /eee/. *The sound* /e/ *is a vowel sound. When you say a vowel sound, you keep your mouth open and let the air flow out. Try it:* /eee/. Then say: *The letter* e *spells the vowel sound* /e/ *you hear in* egg. Point to the *e* and ask: *What is the letter? What is its sound?* Then teach students how to form capital and lowercase *e.*

Practice Have students number a paper from 1–12. For Item 1, say: *What is in this picture? Let's say the word and then its first sound:* bench, /b/. *What letter spells* /b/ *as in* bench? *That's right,* b. Point to the *Bb* on the transparency. Have students write a capital and lowercase *b* by Item 1 on their papers. Repeat the process for Items 2–12.

LANGUAGE AND LITERACY: PHONICS

OBJECTIVES

Learning to Read: Build Oral Vocabulary; Develop Phonemic Awareness; ❶ Associate Letters and Sounds

TEACH LETTERS AND SOUNDS

1 Build Oral Vocabulary Display Transparency 7. Play "I Spy," giving clues until students find the picture. For example, for Item 3, say:

• *I spy a watch. You use a watch to see what time it is. You wear a watch on your wrist* (encircle your wrist).

When students find the watch, say: *Yes,* **this is a watch** (point). Repeat the game to build context for the other words.

2 Develop Phonemic Awareness Remove the transparency and work through Step 1 of the script.

3 Associate Letters and Sounds Display Transparency 7 again. Work through Step 2 of the script.

▶ **Student Journal** pages 47, 48

CLOSE AND ASSESS

Say the words *jar, bench, window, key,* and *egg* one at a time. Have the group write the letter that stands for the first sound in the word on a card and hold it up.

Review and Reteaching
PHONEMIC AWARENESS AND PHONICS

• **Isolate Sounds** Say words that begin with the sounds taught to date and ask students to tell you the first sound they hear in the word. Choose picture names from Transparencies 1, 3, 5, and 7.

• **Match Letters and Sounds** Give one letter card for *j, b, w, k,* or *e* (see pages T33–T38) to five students. Have the other students each draw a picture from the transparency. Then students form groups to match the letters to the first sound in the picture names.

BASIC VOCABULARY AND LANGUAGE DEVELOPMENT

OBJECTIVES

Function: Give Information
Concepts and Vocabulary: 🅣 Body Parts
Patterns and Structures:
🅣 *He/She has* _____.;
🅣 *I/They have* _____.
Viewing: Interpret a Visual Image

USE NAMES FOR BODY PARTS

1 **Look at the Photo** Explain: *It's 12:35 p.m. Carlos is in the nurse's office because he hurt his foot. When you feel sick or get hurt, you can go see the nurse.* Describe the objects in the office: *A cold ice pack can make you feel better.*

2 **Identify Body Parts** Point to the *Parts of the Body* poster in the nurse's office. As you say each word, have students indicate the part on their own bodies.

▶ **Student Journal** page 49

GIVE INFORMATION

3 **Introduce the Patterns:** *He/She has _____.; I/They have* _____. Read aloud the photo captions. Then use a chart to explain the patterns:

Use	To Tell About
I have	yourself
He has	a boy or man
She has	a girl or woman
They have	more than one person

4 **Role-Play** Call on individuals or partners to pantomime the actions in the photos. Then have students use the patterns to describe the feelings: *She has a fever.*

▶ **Student Journal** page 50

CLOSE AND ASSESS

Have students use self-stick notes to write speech balloons for the students on page 21. Model how to convert the caption: *I have a toothache.*

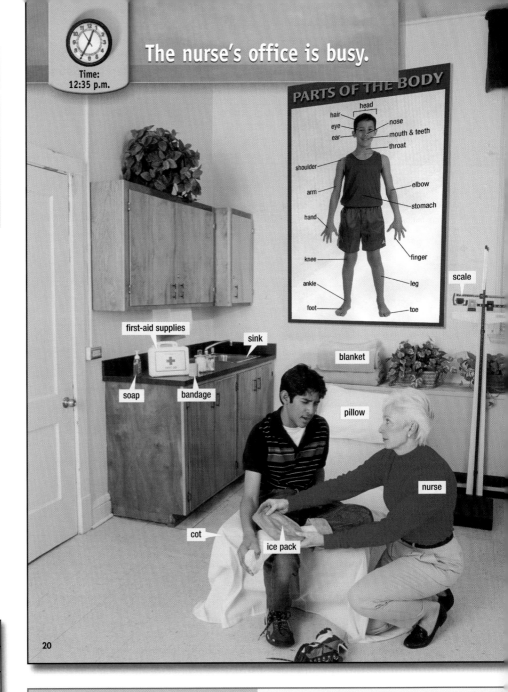

The nurse's office is busy.

Time: 12:35 p.m.

PARTS OF THE BODY

head
hair
eye — nose
ear — mouth & teeth
throat
shoulder
arm — elbow
— stomach
hand
knee
finger
ankle — leg
foot — toe

scale
first-aid supplies
sink
blanket
soap
bandage
pillow
nurse
cot
ice pack

20

REACHING ALL STUDENTS

Vocabulary

BODY PARTS

Hokey Pokey Teach students the gestures to accompany the song "The Hokey Pokey" and sing it together a few times. Then invite students to imitate your actions as you give directions. Sing together a few times and then have student volunteers call out the names of the body parts as the class does the dance.

HOW DO THEY FEEL?

I feel sick.

He has a toothache.

She has a headache.

He has an earache.

She has a stomachache.

thermometer

They have colds.
They have fevers, too.

Listen and Learn

Mrs. Kent:	How do you feel?
Carlos:	My foot hurts. I hurt it in P.E. class.
Mrs. Kent:	I'll put ice on it. You'll feel better tomorrow.
Carlos:	Thank you, Mrs. Kent.

21

OBJECTIVES

Functions: Listen Actively; Repeat Spoken Language; Ask and Answer Questions; Express Feelings (health)

Patterns and Structures:
How do you/they feel?; ❶ *How does he/she feel? I/They feel _____.;* ❶ *He/She feels _____.; My _____ hurt(s).*

Speaking and Representing: Role-Play

ASK QUESTIONS AND EXPRESS FEELINGS (HEALTH)

Side B
CD Track 9

1 **Introduce the Pattern:** *How do you feel?* Play the "Listen and Learn" conversation on the **Lakeside Language Tape/CD.**

2 **Introduce the Patterns:** *I feel _____.* and *My _____ hurt(s).* Ask students: *How do you feel?* Then post a chart of possible responses:

How Do You Feel?

I feel _____.	My _____ hurt(s).
I feel fine.	My head hurts.
I feel sick.	My ears hurt.
I feel better.	My eyes hurt.

3 **Introduce the Patterns:** *How do(es) he/she/they feel?* and *He/She/They feel(s) _____.* Point to the pictures and model how to ask and answer questions: *How does the girl feel? She feels bad.* Point out that for one other person, you use *does;* for more than one, you use *do.*

4 **Use the Patterns** Have volunteers role-play feelings. Then have three students ask and answer questions:

> **Student 1:** How do you feel?
> **Student 2:** My head hurts.
> **Student 3:** She feels sick.

▶ **Student Journal** pages 51, 52

CLOSE AND ASSESS

Call on a student: *Erika, how do you feel?* The student role-plays a feeling and explains: *I feel bad. I have a toothache.*

Language Development
EXPRESS FEELINGS (HEALTH)

Have small groups create skits about going to the school nurse's office. One student can be the nurse and ask: *How do you feel?* The others can use the health-related vocabulary and patterns to express their feelings.

> **Nurse:** How do you feel?
> **Student:** I feel bad. I have a headache.
> **Nurse:** Here is an ice pack.
> **Student:** Thank you. I feel better.

Language Development **T21**

LANGUAGE AND LITERACY: HIGH FREQUENCY WORDS

OBJECTIVES

Learning to Read:
❶ Recognize High Frequency Words

INTRODUCE

1 Learn New Words Place a word and its letter tiles on the screen as you work through the Strategy steps. For example, for *how*, say:

1. *First, look at the word.* (Display the word tile for *how*.)

2. *Now listen to the word:* how, how.

3. *Listen to the word in a sentence:* How do you feel?

4. *Say the word after me:* how.

5. *Spell the word:* h-o-w. (As you say each letter, place the corresponding letter tile. Point to each tile and have students spell the word.)

6. *Say the word again:* how.

Repeat the process for the other words, using these context sentences:

• I **have** a sore foot.
• The nurse **has** ice packs.
• **They** are good for my foot.
• I **put** an ice pack on my foot.
• I **feel** better.

PRACTICE

2 Sort Words Place the word tiles on the screen in a random arrangement. Have students first sort the words by number of letters, and then do a second sort of words that start with *h*.

APPLY

3 Read New Words Have students find the new words on pages 20–21.

▶ **Student Journal** page 53

CLOSE AND ASSESS

Display the words one at a time for students to read.

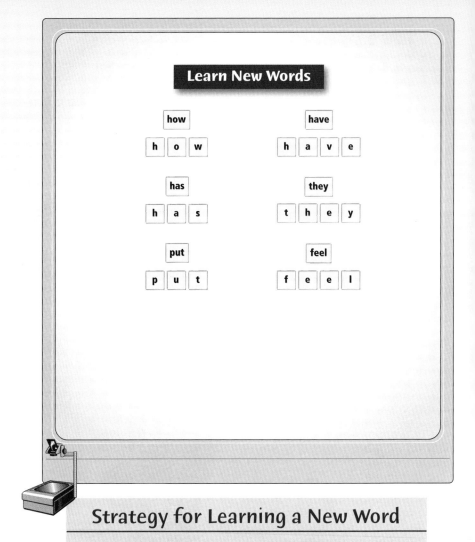

Strategy for Learning a New Word

1. Look at the word.
2. Listen to the word.
3. Listen to the word in a sentence.
4. Say the word.
5. Spell the word.
6. Say the word again.

REACHING ALL STUDENTS

Reading Fluency
RECOGNIZE HIGH FREQUENCY WORDS

To build automaticity with the new high frequency words:

• Use word tiles for new and review words to build sentences on the overhead; for example: *How do they feel? We have a good time. She has a picture of me.* Have students identify the new words and read the sentences.

• Give a volunteer letter tiles for one of the new words. Guide the student in placing one letter at a time to spell the word on the overhead. Others guess the word in as few letters as possible. Whoever guesses finishes the spelling.

Blend Words with Short e

Blend the sounds to read each word.

Ed	men	pet
bed	pen	pat
red	ten	pot

Read each word. Which picture goes with the word?

1. red
2. bed
3. ten
4. pen

A.   B.   C.   D.

Transparency 8   © Hampton-Brown

◄ **Transparency 8: Blending**

Penmanship
For script models and practice in writing words in manuscript or cursive with correct letter spacing, see pages T40–T76.

Materials
Letter tiles for:

a	b	d	e
E	m	n	o
p	r	t	

▼ **Script for Transparency 8**

Blend Words with Short *e*

1. Develop Phonemic Awareness
Create Rhyming Words Say: *Listen to these words:* pet, wet, net. *These words rhyme. They all have the same sounds at the end:* /et/. *Listen again:* pet, wet, net. *Now you say them. Here are three more words that rhyme:* pin, skin, spin. *Now you try. What are some words that rhyme with* nest? (rest, test, chest, best, vest, west) *What words rhyme with* bat? (hat, fat, rat, that, sat, mat, flat, pat)

2. Blend Sounds to Read Words
Model Set letter tile *E* at the left in the box on **Transparency 8** and letter tile *d* at the right. Point to *E* and say: *The sound for this letter is* /eee/. *As you say the sound, slide* E *next to* d, *and then put your finger under* d. Say: *I can blend the sound* /eee/ *with the sound of the letter* d: /eeed/. *Now I'm going to say the word fast:* Ed. Summarize: *You can blend sounds like this to read a word. Just say the sound for the first letter, and blend it into the sound for the next letter.* Demonstrate again: Point to *E* and say: *Say the sound for the letter* E *with me:* /eee/. *Repeat for* d: /d/. *Then slide a finger below the letters* Ed *and say:* Help me blend the two sounds: /eeed/. *Now let's say the word:* Ed. Then replace *E* with *e*, leave *d* at the right in the box, and add letter tile *b* at the left. Repeat the process to read *bed*. Remove the *b* and repeat the process to read *red*.

Practice Have students read the words *Ed, bed,* and *red* below the box. Then repeat Model and Practice for the other two word sets.

3. Match Words and Pictures
Point to Item 1. Say: *Let's read this word.* Slide a finger slowly under the letters to lead students in sounding out the word: /rrreeed/, *red.* Then say: *Now let's look at the pictures. Which of these pictures—A, B, C, or D—shows the color red?* (D) Repeat the process for Items 2, 3, and 4.

LANGUAGE AND LITERACY: PHONICS

OBJECTIVES

Learning to Read: Build Oral Vocabulary; Develop Phonemic Awareness; Blend Sounds to Decode Words

TEACH BLENDING

1 Build Oral Vocabulary Display Transparency 8. Use *men, pet,* and *pat* in sentences to build meaning:

• *One man can lift a chair. Two **men** can lift a table. Do you have a **pet**? I have two **pets**: a dog and a cat. The mother **pats** the baby's back (pantomime).*

Use the pictures to develop the meanings of *red, bed, ten,* and *pen*:

• *This is a **pen**. A **pen** has ink. You write with a **pen**.*

2 Develop Phonemic Awareness Remove the transparency and work through Step 1 of the script.

3 Blend Sounds to Read Words Display Transparency 8 again. Work through Steps 2 and 3 of the script.

▶ **Student Journal** pages 54, 55

CLOSE AND ASSESS

Display *pet, pen, pat, bed,* and *pot*. Call on students to identify the three sounds in each word and then blend the sounds to read the word.

Review and Reteaching
PHONEMIC AWARENESS AND PHONICS

• **Create Rhyming Words** Arrange students in a circle. Choose a word from Transparencies 1–8, for example: *bed*. The two students to your right must agree on a word that rhymes with yours. Go around the circle, encouraging partners to add more rhyming words.

• **Blend Sounds to Decode Words** Distribute letter cards for *e, n, m, p, t, a, i,* and *o* (see pages T33–T38). Have students spell and blend *ten*, then change a letter to spell and blend *men, pen, pet, pat, pit,* and *pot*.

BASIC VOCABULARY AND LANGUAGE DEVELOPMENT

OBJECTIVES

Functions: Listen Actively; Repeat Spoken Language; Express Likes and Dislikes

Concepts and Vocabulary: ❶ Food

Patterns and Structures: *I like _____.;* ❶ *I do not like _____.*

Viewing: Interpret a Visual Image

USE NAMES OF FOODS

1 Introduce Foods Explain: *At 12:45 p.m., Carlos buys lunch at the school cafeteria.* Briefly explain how a cafeteria works: *First, you choose your food. Then you pay the cashier. Then you take the tray to a table and you eat!* Read the food names and have students raise their hands to indicate foods they have tried.

2 Listen for Food Names
Side B
CD Track 10
Play the "Listen and Learn" conversation on the **Lakeside Language Tape/CD**. On the second reading, pause the tape and have students point to the foods as they are mentioned. Then have students echo the conversation and chime in on Carlos's part.

EXPRESS LIKES AND DISLIKES

3 Introduce the Patterns: *I like/do not like _____.* Point to a food on page 23 and model how to express likes and dislikes: *I like pizza. I do not like soup.* Then have volunteers express their preferences.

4 Think, Pair, Share Organize partners for Think, Pair, Share. (see page T94) Students should first think about the foods on page 23, then pair to discuss their likes and dislikes, and share the information with the class.

▶ **Student Journal** page 56

CLOSE AND ASSESS

Name a food and call on students to tell whether or not they like that food.

Time: 12:45 p.m.

What's in the cafeteria?

Listen and Learn

Carlos: How's the food?

Maylin: So-so.

Carlos: What is that on your plate?

Maylin: This is salad. It's not bad.

Carlos: I like pizza and hamburgers.

Maylin: Me, too.

Carlos: I do not like hot dogs.

Maylin: I don't like macaroni and cheese.

Carlos: What's macaroni and cheese?

Maylin: It's sticky and thick. Yuck.

cashier

table

cup

bowl

MONEY

| quarter 25¢ | dime 10¢ | one-dollar bill $1 |
| nickel 5¢ | penny 1¢ | five-dollar bill $5 |

22

REACHING ALL STUDENTS

Vocabulary

FOOD

Food Posters Use the food categories on page 23 to label separate posters. (Hot Food, Salad, etc.) Then divide the class into groups and distribute one poster per group. Students will work together to draw or cut out pictures of foods which fall under their category. Then have group members show their poster and tell about the foods they found: *I like pasta. It is a hot food.*

A CAFETERIA TRAY

straw

tray

milk carton

napkin

chips

paper plate   knife   spoon

fork

HOT FOOD

taco and beans   hot dog   soup   hamburger   macaroni and cheese   pizza

COLD FOOD

cake   apple sauce   bagel   egg   cottage cheese   ice cream

Salad

dressing
tomato
lettuce
carrot

Fruit

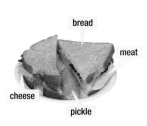

orange
banana
grapes
apple

Sandwich

bread
meat
cheese
pickle

23

Language Development
EXPRESS LIKES AND DISLIKES

Use chart paper to set up a graph with the title "Foods We Like." Have each student choose a picture of a favorite food from **Student Journal** page 57. Sort the pictures and paste them in columns to form a bar graph. Repeat the procedure to create a bar graph for "Foods We Do Not Like." Help students interpret the graphs: *Many people like bagels. A lot of people do not like soup.*

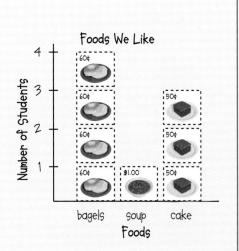

Foods We Like

BASIC VOCABULARY AND LANGUAGE DEVELOPMENT

OBJECTIVES

Functions: Ask for and Give Information
Concepts and Vocabulary: ❶ Money
Patterns and Structures:
What is this/that?; ❶ *This/That is _____.*
Representing: Role-Play

IDENTIFY MONEY

1 Introduce Money Values Show actual coins and bills. Then explain the values:

Coin Name	Value	How Many Make $1.00?
penny	1¢	100

2 Build a Lunch Turn to **Student Journal** page 57 and help students use the pictures to create lunches costing under $2.00. Then ask volunteers to tell about their lunches: *My lunch costs $1.25. I can use a dollar and a quarter to pay.*

▶ **Student Journal** page 57

ASK FOR AND GIVE INFORMATION

3 Introduce the Patterns: *What is this/that?* and *This/That is _____.* Set food items around the room. Explain: *Use* this *to tell about something nearby. Use* that *to tell about something farther away.*

4 Role-Play Set up a cafeteria scene. Students can arrange food pictures from **Student Journal** page 57 to create a lunch on the tray of page 58. Students can ask questions about the food: *What is this food called? What is that?* Cafeteria workers can verify answers by turning over the pictures.

▶ **Student Journal** page 58

CLOSE AND ASSESS

Have partners ask questions such as *What is this food? How much does it cost?*

LANGUAGE AND LITERACY: HIGH FREQUENCY WORDS

OBJECTIVES

Learning to Read:
❶ Recognize High Frequency Words

INTRODUCE

1 **Learn New Words** Place a word and its letter tiles on the screen for the Strategy steps. (See Teacher Note for *don't*.) For example, for *and*, say:

1. *First, look at the word.* (Display the word tile for *and*.)

2. *Now listen to the word:* and, and.

3. *Listen to the word in a sentence:* I like apples and bananas.

4. *Say the word after me:* and.

5. *Spell the word:* a-n-d. (Say each letter as you place the tile. Point to each tile and have students spell the word.)

6. *Say the word again:* and.

Repeat the process for the other words, using these context sentences:

• What **food** do you like to eat?
• **That** is yogurt.
• I do **not** like yogurt.
• I **don't** like beans.

PRACTICE

2 **Build Sentences** Set word tiles randomly and read aloud a sentence: *I like that food.* Place the tile for the first word to the left. Have students tell which tiles go next. Have students read the sentence. Continue with: *We don't like the food. That food is not good.*

APPLY

3 **Read New Words** Have students find the new words on pages 22–23.

▶ **Student Journal** page 59

CLOSE AND ASSESS

Display the words one at a time for students to read.

Learn New Words

| and | food |
| a n d | f o o d |

| that | not |
| t h a t | n o t |

| don't | |
| d o   n o t | |

To spell the word *don't*, close up the words *do not* and remove the second *o*. Then point to the apostrophe in the word tile above and say: *When I close up the words* do not, *I have to put in an apostrophe like you see here.*

Strategy for Learning a New Word

1. Look at the word.
2. Listen to the word.
3. Listen to the word in a sentence.
4. Say the word.
5. Spell the word.
6. Say the word again.

REACHING ALL STUDENTS

Reading Fluency
RECOGNIZE HIGH FREQUENCY WORDS

To build automaticity with the new high frequency words:

• Display the new words. Have partners work together to find and write the three words with *o* or *oo*, the three words with *n*, the three words with *t* at the end, and the three words with *d*.

• Ask a volunteer to look at the classroom chart of new and review words, choose a word, and begin spelling it slowly. The rest of the group should try to guess the word in as few letters as possible.

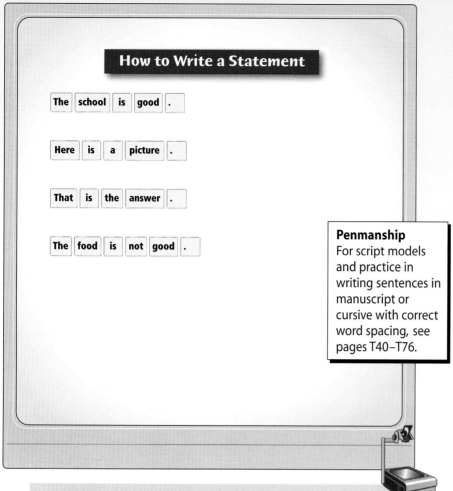

How to Write a Statement

The | school | is | good | .

Here | is | a | picture | .

That | is | the | answer | .

The | food | is | not | good | .

Penmanship
For script models and practice in writing sentences in manuscript or cursive with correct word spacing, see pages T40–T76.

Strategy for Statements

- A statement tells something.
- It starts with a capital letter.
- It ends with a period.

Multi-Level Strategies

CONCEPTS OF PRINT: CAPITAL LETTERS

NON-ROMAN ALPHABET

Students who speak Chinese or another language without capitalization may need practice to remember that a sentence starts with a capital letter. Point out the capital *T* at the beginning of *The school is good.* Display the letter tile for lowercase *t* to show the contrast. Then give partners lowercase letter tiles. Have them match the letters to capital letters at the beginning of sentences on a randomly selected page from pages 4–23.

OBJECTIVES

Writing: ❶ Write a Statement

INTRODUCE

1 Learn About Statements Place the word tiles for the first sentence on the screen as you define a statement. Say:

1. *A statement is a sentence that tells something.* (Display *The school is good,* without the period.)

2. *Listen to the statement.* (As you read, point to each word.)

3. *What does it tell about?* (the school)

4. *The first word starts with a capital letter.* (Point to *T.*) *This is capital* T.

5. *A statement ends with a period.* (Place the period tile at the end.)

6. *Read the statement with me.*

Repeat for the other statements.

PRACTICE

2 Build Sentences Read a statement and place its word tiles randomly.

- They are here.
- We can play.
- It is time to call.
- This food is good.

Have students explain which tile to place first, how to order the rest of the words, and where to place the period. Have them read the statement in unison. Repeat for the other statements.

APPLY

3 Read Statements Have students find statements on pages 4–23.

▶ **Student Journal** page 60

CLOSE AND ASSESS

Provide word tiles for the statements in Step 1. Read each statement and have a volunteer build it. Have other students tell what it is about, point to the capital letter, and point to the period.

BASIC VOCABULARY AND LANGUAGE DEVELOPMENT

OBJECTIVES

Concepts and Vocabulary:
Science Materials and Processes
Viewing: Interpret a Visual Image

USE SCIENCE VOCABULARY

1 **Introduce Science Tools** View pages 24–25 and explain: *It's 1:15 p.m. Carlos is in science class. In the science lab, or laboratory, you can do experiments. They can show how plants grow and how things work.* Point to the objects and describe how they are used: *A model shows how something looks or works. This is a model of the sun and the planets.*

2 **Introduce Science Processes** Read the captions and explain or pantomime each action. Then call on volunteers to pantomime the actions for others to guess.

3 **Visit a School Science Lab** As you examine laboratory equipment, pause for students to check off and add items to the list of science materials at the top of **Student Journal** page 61. Then have them complete the rest of the page.

▶ **Student Journal** page 61

CLOSE AND ASSESS

Ask students questions about science tools and processes, for example:
• *What tool do you use to observe something very small?* (microscope)
• *What do you do with a ruler?* (measure)

Time: 1:15 p.m.

Science class is fun!

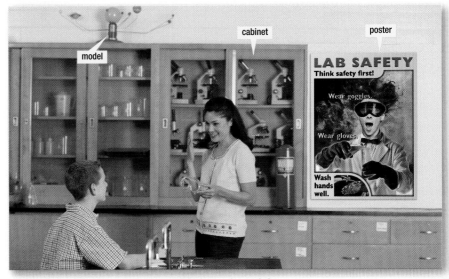

model • cabinet • poster

LAB SAFETY
Think safety first!
Wear goggles.
Wear gloves.
Wash hands well.

This is a science lab.

I listen to the teacher.

report

I do an experiment.

24

REACHING ALL STUDENTS

Vocabulary

SCIENCE TOOLS

Materials per group: one stalk of celery; one cup of water mixed with 2–3 drops of a dark food coloring; graph paper; ruler

Science Experiment Lead small groups in carrying out a simple experiment to show how plants absorb water. Post the following directions, pausing to reinforce the science terms, as needed:

1. **Measure** the level of the water.
2. Put the celery into the cup.
3. **Observe** the changes over time:
   • Measure the water in the cup.
   • Measure the color in the celery.
4. Take **notes**. Write the time, water level, and color level.
5. Show the changes in a line graph.
6. Write a **report**. Tell what you learned.

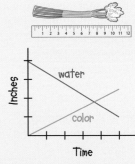

I measure.

microscope
I observe.

notes
I take notes.

Listen and Learn

Carlos:	Mrs. Sato, I need a tray for my plants. Can you give me one?
Mrs. Sato:	I think you need more than one tray!
Carlos:	Yes, I do.
Mrs. Sato:	Then get two trays from the cabinet. Take them to the table.
Carlos:	Thanks.

25

BASIC VOCABULARY AND LANGUAGE DEVELOPMENT

OBJECTIVES

Functions: Listen Actively; Repeat Spoken Language; Express Needs and Thoughts

Patterns and Structures:
❶ I need _____.; I think _____.

EXPRESS NEEDS AND THOUGHTS

Side B
CD
Track 11

1 **Introduce the Patterns:** *I need* _____. and *I think* _____. Play the "Listen and Learn" conversation on the **Lakeside Language Tape/CD**. Students will listen to the conversation twice, then echo the conversation, and chime in on Carlos's part.

2 **Distinguish Between Needs and Thoughts** Explain: *Use* I need *when you have to have something. Use* I think *when you want to share your ideas.* Pantomime measuring a plant, then model the patterns: *I think this plant is growing. Now I need a ruler to measure the plant.*

3 **Think, Pair, Share** Organize partners for Think, Pair, Share. (see page T94) Have students tell about something they need and something they think. Pairs can use the patterns to create two sentences. Show examples in a chart.

I need _____.	I think _____.
some pens a book	you are smart science is fun

▶ **Student Journal** page 62

CLOSE AND ASSESS

Call on students to tell you something they need for school, and something they think about school.

Language Development
EXPRESS NEEDS AND THOUGHTS

Have partners create dialog for one of the scenes on pages 12–25. Encourage them to use the new patterns and others they have learned:

I think _____.

I need _____.

Do you like _____?

I like _____.

I do not like _____.

Encourage volunteers to role-play their dialogs for the group.

LANGUAGE AND LITERACY: HIGH FREQUENCY WORDS

OBJECTIVES

Learning to Read:
➊ Recognize High Frequency Words

INTRODUCE

1 Learn New Words Place a word and its letter tiles on the screen as you work through the Strategy steps. For example, for *think,* say:

1. *First, look at the word.* (Display the word tile for *think*.)

2. *Now listen to the word:* think, think.

3. *Listen to the word in a sentence:* I think science is interesting.

4. *Say the word after me:* think.

5. *Spell the word:* t-h-i-n-k. (As you say each letter, place the corresponding letter tile. Point to each tile and have students spell the word.)

6. *Say the word again:* think.

Repeat the process for the other words, using these context sentences:

- Can you **give** me a tray?
- I **take** the tray to the table.

PRACTICE

2 Build Sentences Set out the word tiles at random and read aloud a sentence: *Take this to school.* Place the tile for the first word to the left. Then have students tell you which tile to place next to arrange the words in order. Have students read the sentence in unison. Continue with: *Can you give me some help? Yes. I think we can.*

APPLY

3 Read New Words Have students find the new words on pages 24–25.

▶ **Student Journal** page 63

CLOSE AND ASSESS

Display the words one at a time for students to read.

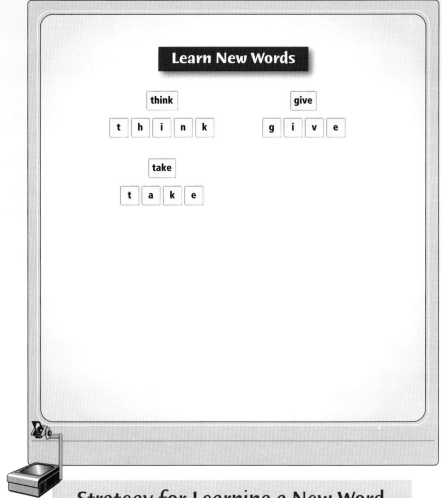

Learn New Words

think   give

t   h   i   n   k   g   i   v   e

take

t   a   k   e

Strategy for Learning a New Word

1. Look at the word.

2. Listen to the word.

3. Listen to the word in a sentence.

4. Say the word.

5. Spell the word.

6. Say the word again.

REACHING ALL STUDENTS

Reading Fluency
RECOGNIZE HIGH FREQUENCY WORDS

To build automaticity with the new high frequency words:

- Use the letter tiles on the overhead to spell the new words, leaving a few letters missing from each one. Have volunteers complete the words and then call on a student to read each word. Repeat the activity, removing different letters from the words.

- Challenge students to create illustrations or pantomime to show the meaning of each new word. Ask them to present a drawing or a performance for the class to guess the word.

Letters and Sounds

◀ Transparency 9:
Letters and Sounds

| Zz | Yy | Uu | QU qu | Xx |

Name each picture. What letter spells the first sound you hear?

1.
2.
3.

Name each picture. What letters spell the first two sounds you hear?

4.
5.
6.

Name each picture. What letter spells the last two sounds you hear?

7.
8.
9.

Transparency 9   © Hampton-Brown

1. upstairs
2. zipper
3. yarn
4. question (mark)
5. quilt
6. quiet
7. box
8. ox
9. ax

Penmanship
For script models and practice in manuscript or cursive letter formations, see pages T40–T76.

▼ **Script for Transparency 9**

Letters and Sounds

1. Develop Phonemic Awareness
Match/Identify Sounds Say: *Listen to these two words:* zoo, zebra. *Do they begin with the same sound?* (yes) Repeat with: *yawn, yarn; zipper, zero; umbrella, envelope; up, yes.* Next, have students identify the first two sounds in *queen, quick, quilt.* (/kw/) Repeat for the last two sounds in *six, box, fix.* (/ks/)

2. Associate Letters and Sounds
Learn the Name, Sound, and Formation for the Vowel Uu Point to *Uu* on **Transparency 9** and say: *This is the letter* u—*capital* U *and lowercase* u. *The letter* u *is a* **vowel**. Point to the umbrella and say: *Say* umbrella *with me:* umbrella. *Say its first sound:* /uuu/. *The sound* /uuu/ *is a vowel sound.* Explain: *When you say a vowel sound, you keep your mouth open and let the air flow out. Try it:* /uuu/. *The letter* u *spells the vowel sound* /u/ *in* umbrella. Point to the *u* and ask: *What is the letter? What is its sound?* Then teach students how to form capital and lowercase *u.*

Learn Consonant Names, Sounds, and Formations Point to the zero. Say: *This is zero. Zero is a number that stands for none. Say* zero *with me:* zero. Then point to *Zz* and say: *This is capital* Z, *and this is lowercase* z. *The letter* z *spells the first sound you hear in* zero. *The first sound is* /z/. *Say* /zzz/ *with me:* /zzz/. Point to the *z* and ask: *What is the letter? What is its sound?* Trace the *Zz* on the transparency as you explain how to form the letters and have students "write" the letters in the air. Repeat for *y, qu,* and *x.* Explain: *The letters* z, y, q, *and* x *are called* **consonants**—*they spell consonant sounds.*

Practice Have students number a paper from 1–12. For Item 1, say: *Let's say this word and its first sound:* upstairs, /uuu/. *What letter spells* /uuu/ *as in* upstairs? (u) Point to the *Uu.* Have students write a capital and lowercase *u* by Item 1 on their papers. Repeat for Items 2–3. For Items 4–6, have students identify the first two sounds in each word (/kw/) and write the letters that stand for those sounds. For Items 7–9, have students identify the last two sounds in each word (/ks/) and write the letter that stands for those sounds.

LANGUAGE AND LITERACY: PHONICS

OBJECTIVES

Learning to Read: Build Oral Vocabulary; Develop Phonemic Awareness; **T** Associate Letters and Sounds

TEACH LETTERS AND SOUNDS

1 Build Oral Vocabulary Display Transparency 9. Play "I Spy," giving clues until students find the picture. For example, for Item 2, say:

- *I spy a zipper. You move a zipper to open and close a jacket.*

Say: *Yes,* **this is the zipper** (point). Repeat the game for the other words.

2 Develop Phonemic Awareness Remove the transparency and work through Step 1 of the script.

3 Associate Letters and Sounds Display Transparency 9 again. Work through Step 2 of the script.

▶ **Student Journal** pages 64, 65

CLOSE AND ASSESS

Say the words *zipper, umbrella* and *yarn* one at a time. Have the group write the letter that stands for the first sound in the word on a card and hold it up. Repeat for the letters that make the first two sounds in *quilt* (qu) and the letter that makes the last two sounds in *six.*

Review and Reteaching
PHONEMIC AWARENESS AND PHONICS

- **Isolate Sounds** Say words that begin with the sounds taught to date and ask students to tell you the first sound they hear in the word. Choose picture names from Transparencies 1, 3, 5, 7, and 9. For words with /kw/ *qu* or /ks/ *x,* ask students to tell you the first two or last two sounds they hear.

- **Match Letters and Sounds** Display Transparencies 1, 3, 5, 7, and 9 to reteach the letters and sounds. Help students create a word file where they collect words for each letter and sound.

BASIC VOCABULARY AND LANGUAGE DEVELOPMENT

OBJECTIVES

Concepts and Vocabulary:
❶ Clothing; Colors
Viewing: Interpret a Visual Image

USE WORDS FOR COLORS AND CLOTHING

1 Identify Colors Explain: *It's 3:15 p.m., and Carlos is shopping in the school store. He can buy school supplies and clothes there.* Call attention to the color chart. Present the names of the colors, then have students name colors they see around the room.

2 Identify Articles of Clothing Say the name of each item of clothing on page 27. Have students give the name and color of items they can identify in the store display on page 26: *I see a tan sweatshirt.*

3 Play "I Spy" Give clues using words for colors and articles of clothing: *I spy blue socks.* All students wearing blue socks stand up. Ask a volunteer to give the next clue, and continue until all students have a chance to speak.

▶ **Student Journal** page 66

CLOSE AND ASSESS

Have students describe what their partner is wearing while the partner "models" or points to each item.

The school store has good things!

Time: 3:15 p.m.

These T-shirts are nice!

The Lakeside Lions T-shirt comes in 11 great colors!

yellow	green	● black
orange	blue	gray
red	purple	○ white
pink	tan	

I like those little lions.

26

REACHING ALL STUDENTS

Vocabulary
COLORS AND CLOTHING

Fashion Show Have small groups organize fashion shows. Students can take turns modeling and describing the items of clothing: *This is a blue school sweatshirt. Here are some red pants.* Students may videotape the fashion shows and play them for families or other classes.

CULTURAL PERSPECTIVES

World Cultures: Traditional Costumes Encourage students to describe traditional clothing from their home cultures. Students can bring in photos or articles of clothing to share with the class. Then invite family members to participate in a fashion show of regional, traditional, and ceremonial clothing. Encourage students to narrate as family members "model."

WHICH CLOTHES DO YOU LIKE?

gray sweatshirt

white cap

red jacket

tan T-shirt

blue shorts

green sweatpants

black sneakers

purple socks

Listen and Learn

Maylin: You can get good things at this store! Look at this little Lakeside lion.

Carlos: I like its T-shirt! I need a new T-shirt, too. Do you like this one?

Maylin: No, I don't like that color. I do like those blue shorts.

Carlos: I like them too. My gym shorts are very old. I will get both the T-shirt and the shorts!

Maylin: I will just get my lion.

27

BASIC VOCABULARY AND LANGUAGE DEVELOPMENT

OBJECTIVES

Functions: Listen Actively; Repeat Spoken Language; Ask and Answer Questions

Patterns and Structures: *Which _____ do you like?; I like this/that _____.; I like these/those _____.*

ASK AND ANSWER QUESTIONS

Materials: various articles of clothing in different colors

Side B
CD
Track 12

1 **Introduce the Patterns:** *I like this/that ___.; I like these/those ___.* Play the "Listen and Learn" conversation on the **Lakeside Language Tape/CD**. Students will listen twice to the conversation, echo lines, and chime in with Carlos.

Use page 26 to explain how to choose the correct demonstrative adjective:

	one	more than one
near	**this** hat	**these** shoes
far	**that** shirt	**those** socks

Use the patterns to describe classroom objects: *I like that poster on the wall. I like these pens in my hand.*

2 **Introduce the Pattern:** *Which _____ do you like?* Explain that you use the pattern to get someone to choose from a group the things they like the most. Ask volunteers to choose clothes they like from page 27.

3 **Use the Patterns to Ask and Answer Questions** Set out several items of clothing. Have one partner ask questions: *Which cap do you like?* The other partner points and uses the patterns to answer: *I like this cap.*

▶ **Student Journal** page 67

CLOSE AND ASSESS

Divide students into groups of three. One student asks a question with *Which _____ do you like?* The others answer by naming objects that are near or farther away.

Language Development
ASK AND ANSWER QUESTIONS

Set up a simulation of a school store using personal and/or classroom objects. Students can take turns being the store clerk and customers. Provide sentence frames for students to ask and answer questions about sale items:

Which _____ do you like?
I like/do not like _____.
I like this/that _____.
I like these/those _____.
I need/think _____.
Here is/are _____.

OBJECTIVES

Learning to Read:
❶ Recognize High Frequency Words

INTRODUCE

1 Learn New Words Place a word and its letter tiles on the screen as you work through the Strategy steps. For example, for *very*, say:

1. *First, look at the word.* (Display the word tile for *very*.)

2. *Now listen to the word:* very, very.

3. *Listen to the word in a sentence:* This is a very good store.

4. *Say the word after me:* very.

5. *Spell the word:* v-e-r-y. (As you say each letter, place the corresponding letter tile. Point to each tile and have students spell the word.)

6. *Say the word again:* very.

Repeat the process for the other words, using these context sentences:

• I will **get** some **things** at the store.
• **These little** erasers are nicer than my **old** ones.
• I want **both** of **them**.
• **Which** bags do you like?
• I like **those** gray bags over there.

PRACTICE

2 Sort Words Place the word tiles on the screen in a random arrangement. Have students sort the words by the number of letters, and then do a second sort of words that start with the letters *th*.

APPLY

3 Read New Words Have students find the new words on pages 26–27.

▶ **Student Journal** page 68

CLOSE AND ASSESS

Display the words one at a time for students to read.

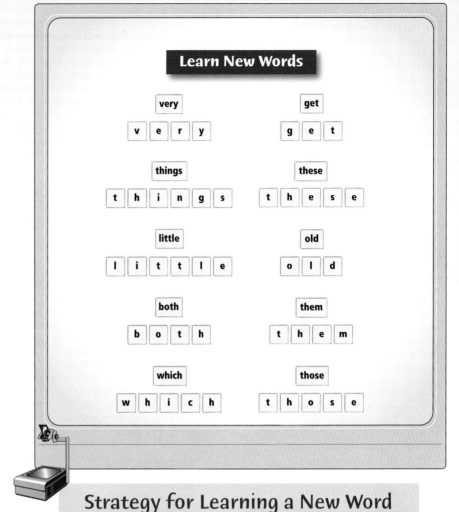

Learn New Words

very	get
things	these
little	old
both	them
which	those

Strategy for Learning a New Word

1. Look at the word.
2. Listen to the word.
3. Listen to the word in a sentence.

4. Say the word.
5. Spell the word.
6. Say the word again.

REACHING ALL STUDENTS

Reading Fluency
RECOGNIZE HIGH FREQUENCY WORDS

To build automaticity with the new high frequency words:

• Have small groups secretly choose five words to make cards for, cut the letters apart, and scramble the letters for each word. Then groups trade sets of letters and compete to see which group can reassemble and read their words faster.

• Invite students to list the words in different ways; for example: alphabetical order or shortest to longest. Ask students to share their lists and have others guess the reason for the ordering.

Blend Words with Short u

Blend the sounds to read each word.

up	us	cut
cup	bus	cat
pup	Gus	cot

Read each word. Which picture goes with the word?

1. bus
2. cot
3. cup
4. cat

A.   B.   C.   D.

© Hampton-Brown

◀ **Transparency 10: Blending**

Penmanship
For script models and practice in writing words in manuscript or cursive with correct letter spacing, see pages T40–T76.

Materials
Letter tiles for:

a	b	c	G	o
p	p	s	t	u

▼ **Script for Transparency 10**

Blend Words with Short *u*

1. Develop Phonemic Awareness

Match Initial Sounds/Match Final Sounds Say: *Listen to these two words:* up, us. *Say the words with me:* up, us. *The first sound in these words is the same:* /uuu/. *Now listen to these two words:* us, am. *Say the words with me:* us, am. *Is the first sound in each word the same?* (no) Continue with word pairs *us, is; yes, yell; cap, cut.* Then say: *Now listen to these two words:* cup, nap. *Say the words with me:* cup, nap. *They end with the same sound:* /p/. *Here are two more words:* bus, cut. *Say the words with me:* bus, cut. *Is the last sound in each word the same?* (no) Continue with word pairs *cup, cot; cut, cat; gas, bus; net, cab; bag, pig.*

2. Blend Sounds to Read Words

Model Set letter tile *u* at the left in the box on **Transparency 10** and letter tile *p* at the right. Point to *u* and say: *The sound for this letter is /uuu/.* As you say the sound, slide *u* next to *p*, and then put your finger under *p*. Say: *I can blend the sound /uuu/ with the sound of the letter* p: /uuup/. *Now I'm going to say the word fast:* up. Summarize: *You can blend sounds like this to read a word. Just say the sound for the first letter, and blend it into the sound for the next letter.* Demonstrate again: Point to *u* and say: *Say the sound for* u *with me:* /uuu/. Repeat for *p*: /p/. Then slide a finger below the letters *up* and say: *Help me blend the two sounds:* /uuup/. *Now let's say the word:* up. Then leave *up* at the right in the box and add letter tile *c* at the left. Repeat the process to read *cup*. Remove the *c* and repeat the process to read *pup*.

Practice Have students read the words *up, cup,* and *pup* below the box. Then repeat Model and Practice for the other two word sets.

3. Match Words and Pictures

Point to Item 1. Say: *Let's read this word.* Slide a finger slowly under the letters to lead students in sounding out the word: /buuusss/, *bus.* Then say: *Now let's look at the pictures. Which of these pictures—A, B, C, or D—shows a bus?* (C) Repeat the process for Items 2, 3, and 4.

LANGUAGE AND LITERACY: PHONICS

OBJECTIVES

Learning to Read: Build Oral Vocabulary; Develop Phonemic Awareness; Blend Sounds to Decode Words

TEACH BLENDING

1 Build Oral Vocabulary Display Transparency 10. Use *pup, us,* and *cut* in sentences to build meaning:

- *My friend's dog had puppies. She gave* **us**—*my sister and me*—*one* **pup**. *I use a knife to* **cut** *bread* (pantomime).

Use the pictures to develop the meaning of *cot, cup, bus,* and *cat:*

- *This is a* **cot**. *A* **cot** *is a small bed. When you are sick, you can lie down on a* **cot** *in the first aid room.*

2 Develop Phonemic Awareness Remove the transparency and work through Step 1 of the script.

3 Blend Sounds to Read Words Display Transparency 10 again. Work through Steps 2 and 3 of the script.

▶ **Student Journal** pages 69, 70

CLOSE AND ASSESS

Display *bus, cup, cot, cut,* and *cap*. Have students identify the sound of each letter and blend the sounds to read the word.

Review and Reteaching
PHONEMIC AWARENESS AND PHONICS

- **Create Rhyming Words** Arrange students in a circle. Choose a word from Transparencies 1–10, for example: *cap, pet,* or *mop*. The two students to your right must agree on a word that rhymes with yours. Go around the circle, encouraging partners to add more rhyming words.

- **Blend Sounds to Decode Words** Distribute letter cards for *a, p, p, c, u, b, i,* and *t* (see pages T33–T38). Have students spell and blend *up,* then add a letter or change a letter to spell and blend *pup, cup, cut, but, bit,* and *bat*.

BASIC VOCABULARY AND LANGUAGE DEVELOPMENT

OBJECTIVES

Concepts and Vocabulary:
Days of the Week
Viewing: Interpret a Visual Image

USE NAMES FOR DAYS OF THE WEEK

1 Introduce the Days of the Week Use a calendar to explain: *There are seven days in one week. The weekdays are Monday through Friday. The weekend is Saturday and Sunday.* Write the days on separate index cards and invite volunteers to put them in order.

2 Play a Game Call out a day of the week: *Tuesday.* Then toss an object to a student, who names the day that follows: *Wednesday.* Play continues until the players review the days for one week.

3 Discuss Daily Activities Explain: *There are many things to do this week.* Point to the sign on page 28 and read the days and events. Ask: *When is the teacher meeting?* (Tuesday) *What will happen on Sunday?* (car wash)

4 Introduce Abbreviations Explain that, to save space in writing, people sometimes use a shorter form of a word, known as an **abbreviation**. Present the following abbreviations:

Sunday	Sun.	Thursday	Thurs.
Monday	Mon.	Friday	Fri.
Tuesday	Tue.	Saturday	Sat.
Wednesday	Wed.		

Point out that these abbreviations are formed from the first few letters of the word plus a period. To practice, write an abbreviation on the board and have a volunteer call out the day.

▶ **Student Journal** page 71

CLOSE AND ASSESS

Have students name a day of the week and tell something they do on that day: *I have piano lessons on Wednesday.*

Time: 3:30 p.m.

Lakeside School is great!

Bye! See you soon!

See you later

SCHOOL SIGN

LAKESIDE LIONS

LAKESIDE SCHOOL

THE FIRST WEEK AT LAKESIDE:

MONDAY: WELCOME BACK!

TUESDAY: TEACHER MEETING

WEDNESDAY: BACK-TO-SCHOOL NIGHT

THURSDAY: SCIENCE CLUB

FRIDAY: WELCOME BACK DANCE

SATURDAY: FOOTBALL GAME

SUNDAY: SOCCER TEAM CAR WASH

28

REACHING ALL STUDENTS

Vocabulary
DAYS OF THE WEEK

School Signs Have small groups make school signs similar to the one on page 28. Suggest classroom or school-wide events they can include. Post the signs on a bulletin board and lead the class in reading each one aloud. At the end of each day, invite a student to tell about upcoming events: *On Wednesday, the science report is due. On Friday, we have a basketball game.*

Room 256
Mountain View School

This week in Room 256:
Monday: Report Cards
Tuesday: Soccer Game
Wednesday: Science Report due
Thursday: Library
Friday: Basketball Game
Saturday: School Dance
Sunday: Math Club Picnic

Good-bye!

See you Tuesday!

So long!

Listen and Learn 🔊

Maylin:	How do you like Lakeside School?
Carlos:	I like it a lot! There is a lot to do.
Maylin:	Yes, there is! On Friday there is a big dance. Do you want to go?
Carlos:	Yes!
Maylin:	Great! I'll see you tomorrow.
Carlos:	Okay. Good-bye!

29

Language Development
EXPRESS SOCIAL COURTESIES

Have small groups review the social courtesies they have learned. Create a class chart of words and phrases:

Greetings	Introductions	Good-byes
Hello!	I am ——.	Bye!
Hi!	My name is	See you
Nice to	——.	later!
meet you.	This is my	See you
	friend ——.	Tuesday!

Then invite volunteers to use the social courtesies to role-play student conversations on the first day of school.

BASIC VOCABULARY AND LANGUAGE DEVELOPMENT

OBJECTIVES

Functions: Listen Actively; Repeat Spoken Language; Express Social Courtesies

Patterns and Structures: *See you ——.*

EXPRESS SOCIAL COURTESIES

1 **Introduce Ways to Say Good-bye** Point to the picture on pages 28–29 and explain: *The students are going home. They use different ways to say good-bye.* Read aloud the speech balloons. Then play the "Listen and Learn" conversation on the **Lakeside Language Tape/CD**. Students will listen to the conversation twice as they follow along. As the tape continues, students will echo the conversation and then chime in on Carlos's part.

Side B
CD Track 13

2 **Use the Pattern: *See you ——.*** Brainstorm ways to complete the pattern using time words or phrases:

> See you ——.
>
> See you soon.
> See you later.
> See you tomorrow.
> See you Monday.
> See you next week.

Use one of the phrases and call on students to answer by using another phrase that means good-bye.

▶ **Student Journal** page 72

CLOSE AND ASSESS

As students leave the room, have them say good-bye using the words, phrases, and patterns on the page.

LANGUAGE AND LITERACY: HIGH FREQUENCY WORDS

OBJECTIVES

Learning to Read:
❶ Recognize High Frequency Words

INTRODUCE

1 Learn New Words Place a word and its letter tiles on the screen as you work through the Strategy steps. For example, for *soon*, say:

1. *First, look at the word.* (Display the word tile for *soon*.)

2. *Now listen to the word:* soon, soon.

3. *Listen to the word in a sentence:* A basketball game will start soon.

4. *Say the word after me:* soon.

5. *Spell the word:* s-o-o-n. (As you say each letter, place the corresponding letter tile. Point to each tile and have students spell the word.)

6. *Say the word again:* soon.

Repeat the process for the other words, using these context sentences:

- There is a soccer game **tomorrow**.
- I'll practice **later** this afternoon.
- Have a **great** game!

PRACTICE

2 Build Sentences Set out the word tiles at random and read aloud a sentence: *I can see you soon.* Place the tile for the first word to the left. Then have students tell you which tiles to place next. Have students read the sentence in unison. Continue with: *I can see you tomorrow. I can call you later. This school is great!*

APPLY

3 Read New Words Have students find the new words on pages 28–29.

▶ **Student Journal** page 73

CLOSE AND ASSESS

Display the words one at a time for students to read.

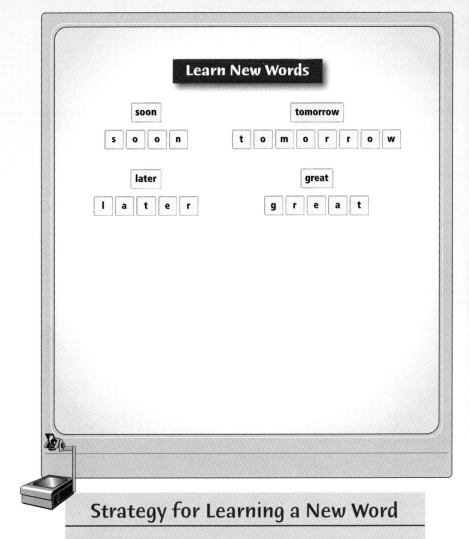

Learn New Words

soon
s o o n

tomorrow
t o m o r r o w

later
l a t e r

great
g r e a t

Strategy for Learning a New Word

1. Look at the word.
2. Listen to the word.
3. Listen to the word in a sentence.
4. Say the word.
5. Spell the word.
6. Say the word again.

REACHING ALL STUDENTS

Multimodal Practice
RECOGNIZE HIGH FREQUENCY WORDS

Display the sentences from Step 2. Then do the following activities.

Kinesthetic Students copy the sentences onto strips and cut them apart to make word and punctuation cards.

Visual Students reassemble the sentences to match those displayed.

Auditory Students work with partners to practice saying the sentences naturally, and then perform or tape a final reading for the class to hear.

How to Write a Question

| How | do | you | feel | ? |

| Where | is | the | picture | ? |

| What | time | is | it | ? |

| Can | you | play | tomorrow | ? |

Penmanship
For script models and practice in writing sentences in manuscript or cursive with correct word spacing, see pages T40–T76.

Strategy for Questions

- A question asks something.
- It starts with a capital letter.
- It ends with a question mark.

- These words can start a question: *Are, Can, Do, Does, How, Is, What, Which, Where, Who, Will.*

Multi-Level Strategies
CONCEPTS OF PRINT: PUNCTUATION

LITERATE IN L1 Some languages follow different print conventions. For example: Spanish uses an inverted question mark before a question, as well as a question mark at the end. Arabic uses a question mark only at the beginning of a question. Have students work with a set of statements and questions copied out of Lakeside pages 4–29, without the end punctuation. Partners can add a period or a question mark to punctuate each sentence. Remind them that English uses a question mark only at the end of a question.

LANGUAGE AND LITERACY: QUESTIONS

OBJECTIVES

Writing: ❶ Write a Question

INTRODUCE

1 **Learn About Questions** Place the word tiles for the first sentence on the screen as you define a question. Say:

1. *A question is a sentence that asks something.* (Display *How do you feel,* without the question mark.)

2. *Listen to the question.* (Point to each word as you read *How do you feel?*)

3. *What does it ask about?* (feelings)

4. *The first word starts with a capital letter.* (Point to *H.*) *This is capital* H.

5. *A question ends with a question mark.* (Place the question mark.)

6. *Read the question with me.*

Repeat for the other questions.

PRACTICE

2 **Build Questions** Read a question and place its word tiles randomly: *What is your name? Who is she? Are they at school? Do you like the picture?*

Have students explain which word to place first, how to order the rest of the words, and where to place the question mark. Have them read the question in unison. Repeat for the other questions.

APPLY

3 **Read Questions** Have students find examples of questions on pages 6–29.

▶ **Student Journal** page 74

CLOSE AND ASSESS

Provide word tiles for the questions in Step 1. Read each question and have a volunteer build it. Have other students tell what it asks about, point to the capital letter, and point to the question mark.

BASIC VOCABULARY AND LANGUAGE DEVELOPMENT

OBJECTIVES

Concepts and Vocabulary:
Months of the Year

Critical Thinking:
Analyze Information; Generate Ideas

Representing: Graph; Calendar

USE NAMES FOR THE MONTHS OF THE YEAR

Materials: 12-month calendar

1 **Introduce the Months of the Year**
Use a calendar to explain the months of the year: *There are twelve months in a year. January is the first month.* Say the names of the months in order as you page through the calendar.

2 **Conduct a Survey** Call out the names of the months in order and have students raise their hands to indicate the month of their birthdays. Have students help you tally the responses.

3 **Analyze Information** Display the results of the birthday survey in the form of a bar graph. Go over the data together; for example: *What month has the most/least birthdays? How many students were born in May?*

4 **Record Monthly Activities** Have students use **Student Journal** page 75 to make a personal calendar. Students should draw a picture and write a sentence describing something they do each month. Then they can share their work in small groups.

▶ **Student Journal** page 75

CLOSE AND ASSESS

Have partners alternate saying the names of the months in order.

Carlos has a great year!

September
Carlos meets lots of new friends.

October
Carlos sees a football game at night.

January
Carlos takes a picture of the snow.

February
Carlos gets a valentine from a girl in his class!

May
Carlos dances with a group at the school dance.

June
Carlos takes final exams.

30

REACHING ALL STUDENTS

HOME CONNECTION

Family Calendar Have students take home **Student Journal** page 75 and explain their drawings and sentences to family members. Then students can help create a family calendar containing important family dates and events. Students can report back to the class about how the family used the calendar, or bring the calendar in to share.

November
Carlos writes letters to his family.

> November 13
> Dear Grandma and Grandpa,
>   I really like it here at
> Lakeside School. I have met lots
> of new friends. I have great
> teachers, too. My favorite subject
> is math. I miss you.
>   Love,
>   Carlos

March
Carlos works in the school garden one day a week.

July
Carlos visits St. Louis.

The Saint Louis Arch

St. Louis, Missouri

December
Carlos sings songs from a book.

April
Carlos plays softball.

August
Carlos swims at the city pool with a boy from his class.

31

Language Development
THIRD PERSON SINGULAR VERBS

Have small groups make up skits about what they do all year, using the months of the year and action verbs. One student narrates as the others act. Provide examples:

> *In February, Miriam plays in the snow. Bao eats moon cakes.*

You might also assign three months to each of four groups and put all the skits together to make one play.

BASIC VOCABULARY AND LANGUAGE DEVELOPMENT

OBJECTIVES

Functions: Listen Actively; Repeat Spoken Language; Describe Actions
Concepts and Vocabulary:
❶ Action Verbs
Patterns and Structures:
Present Tense Verbs

USE THIRD PERSON SINGULAR VERBS

1 View the Photographs Explain: *These photos show what Carlos does each month of the year.* Call out the names of the months and read aloud the captions as students point to the correct picture.

2 Introduce Action Verbs Ask students to perform actions such as *run, walk, sit, stand, sing, read.* As students complete the actions, write sentences to describe them:

> Mai runs.
> Ali talks.
> Javier sits.
> Gina stands.

Underline the *-s* at the end of each verb and explain: *When you describe one person's actions, use an -s at the end of the action word.* Read the sentences aloud and have students echo.

3 Use Action Verbs Have students take the role of Carlos and pantomime an action from one of the pages. Others should guess the action, to complete the sentence *Carlos _____.*

▶ **Student Journal** pages 76, 77

CLOSE AND ASSESS

Have volunteers show their drawings and read their sentences from the bottom of **Student Journal** page 77. Call on someone else to tell the action word in each sentence.

LANGUAGE AND LITERACY: HIGH FREQUENCY WORDS

OBJECTIVES

Learning to Read:
❶ Recognize High Frequency Words

INTRODUCE

1 Learn New Words Place a word and its letter tiles on the screen as you work through the Strategy steps. For example, for *boy*, say:

1. *First, look at the word.* (Display the word tile for *boy*.)

2. *Now listen to the word:* boy, boy.

3. *Listen to the word in a sentence:* Carlos is a boy.

4. *Say the word after me:* boy.

5. *Spell the word:* b-o-y. (Say each letter as you place the tile. Point to each tile and have students spell the word.)

6. *Say the word again:* boy.

Repeat the process for the other words, using these context sentences:

• Every **day** Carlos reads a **book**.
• He does his homework at **night** with a **group** of friends.
• He writes **letters** to a **girl**.
• May is the best time of the **year**!

PRACTICE

2 Sort Words Place the word tiles randomly. Have students sort the words into words that name a person, words that name a time, and words that name one or more things. (person: *boy, girl*; time: *day, night, year*; thing or things: *book, letters, group*)

APPLY

3 Read New Words Have students find the new words on pages 30–31.

▶ **Student Journal** page 78

CLOSE AND ASSESS

Display the words one at a time for students to read.

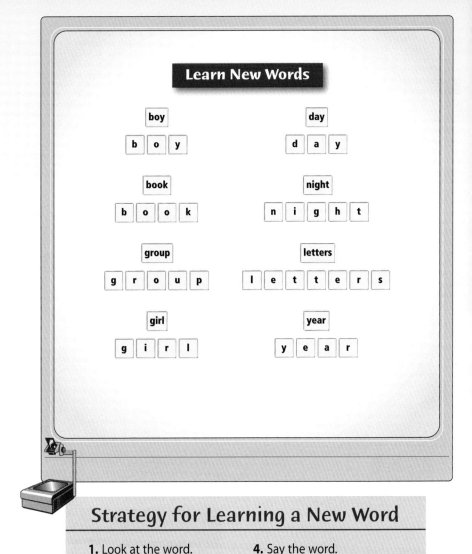

Learn New Words

boy — b o y
day — d a y
book — b o o k
night — n i g h t
group — g r o u p
letters — l e t t e r s
girl — g i r l
year — y e a r

Strategy for Learning a New Word

1. Look at the word.
2. Listen to the word.
3. Listen to the word in a sentence.
4. Say the word.
5. Spell the word.
6. Say the word again.

REACHING ALL STUDENTS

Reading Fluency
RECOGNIZE HIGH FREQUENCY WORDS

To build automaticity with the new high frequency words:

• Have students create memory aids to cue meaning and/or pronunciation of the words. For example, for *day*, they might show the sun rising to cue meaning or write "d-A-y" to help with pronunciation.

• The words in this lesson often appear on charts, signs, lists, posters, and bulletin boards around school. Invite partners to go on a high frequency word hunt. Have them record the number of times and where they find each word. Later, sets of partners can compare their findings.

How to Write an Exclamation

| You | do | great | work | ! |

| I | like | this | book | ! |

| I | see | some | good | food | ! |

| They | play | day | and | night | ! |

Penmanship
For script models and practice in writing sentences in manuscript or cursive with correct word spacing, see pages T40–T76.

Strategy for Exclamations

- An exclamation shows a strong feeling.
- It starts with a capital letter.
- It ends with an exclamation mark.

Multi-Level Strategies
CONCEPTS OF PRINT: PUNCTUATION

LITERATE IN L1 Some languages follow different print conventions. For example: Spanish uses an inverted exclamation mark before an exclamation, as well as an exclamation mark at the end. Have students work with a set of statements, questions, and exclamations copied out of Lakeside pages 4–31, without the end punctuation. Partners can add a period, a question mark, or an exclamation mark to punctuate each sentence. Remind them that English uses these marks only as end punctuation.

LANGUAGE AND LITERACY: EXCLAMATIONS

OBJECTIVES
Writing:
❶ Write an Exclamation

INTRODUCE

1 Learn About Exclamations Place the word tiles for the first sentence on the screen. Say:

1. *An exclamation is a sentence that shows a strong feeling.* (Display *You do great work,* without the exclamation mark.)

2. *Listen to the exclamation:* (Point to each word as you read: *You do great work!*)

3. *Does this sentence show a strong feeling?* (yes)

4. *The first word starts with a capital letter.* (Point to *Y.*) *This is capital Y.*

5. *An exclamation ends with an exclamation mark.* (Place the tile for the exclamation mark at the end.)

6. *Read the exclamation with me.*

Repeat for the other exclamations.

PRACTICE

2 Build Sentences Read a sentence and place its word tiles and exclamation mark randomly: *I think you are great! This book is very old! I need help! We can play here!* Have students tell you how to arrange the words and exclamation mark. Then have them read the exclamation in unison. Repeat for the other sentences.

APPLY

3 Read Exclamations Have students find exclamations on pages 10–31.

▶ **Student Journal** page 79

CLOSE AND ASSESS

Provide word tiles for the exclamations in Step 1. Read each exclamation and have a volunteer build it. Have other students name the feeling and point to the capital letter and exclamation mark.

Teacher Resources

A	A	A	a	a	a
E	E	E	e	e	e
e	e	e	I	I	I
i	i	i	i	i	i

O	O	O	O	o	o
o	o	o	U	U	U
u	u	u	u	u	u
B	B	B	b	b	b
C	C	C	c	c	c

D	D	D	d	d	d
F	F	F	f	f	f
G	G	G	g	g	g
H	H	H	h	h	h
J	J	J	j	j	j

K	K	K	k	k	k
L	L	L	l	l	l
M	M	M	m	m	m
N	N	N	n	n	n
P	P	P	p	p	p

Q	Q	Q	q	q	q
R	R	R	r	r	r
S	S	S	s	s	s
T	T	T	t	t	t
V	V	V	v	v	v

Letter Cards **T37**

W W W w w w

X X X x x x

Y Y Y y y y

Z Z Z z z z

Handwriting Scripts and Practice Sheets

Scripts for Letter Formation

Lowercase Manuscript Letters

Begin with your pencil on the number 1 just below the middle line and follow the arrow to make a circle. Without picking up your pencil, continue up to the middle line and then follow the arrow down to the bottom line. Stop. That's lowercase a. Try it again.

Begin with your pencil on the number 1 at the top line and follow the arrow down to the bottom line. Without picking up your pencil, follow the arrow up and go over that line. Just before you reach the middle line, curve around, touching the middle line, and then down to the bottom line. Stop. That's lowercase h. Try it again.

Begin with your pencil on the number 1 at the top line and follow the arrow down to the bottom line. Without picking up your pencil, go back up over the line you just made to just below the middle line. Follow the arrow to make a circle. Stop. That's lowercase b. Try it again.

Begin with your pencil on the number 1 at the middle line and follow the arrow down to the bottom line. Pick up your pencil and put it on the number 2 and make a dot. Stop. That's lowercase i. Try it again.

Begin with your pencil on the number 1 just below the middle line and follow the arrow around in a circle, touching the middle line and the bottom line as you curve around. Stop a little above the bottom line. That's lowercase c. Try it again.

Begin with your pencil on the number 1 at the middle line and follow the arrow down past the bottom line and curve up to make a little hook. Pick up your pencil and put it on the number 2 and make a dot. Stop. That's lowercase j. Try it again.

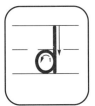

Begin with your pencil on the number 1 just below the middle line and follow the arrow to make a circle. Without picking up your pencil, continue up to the top line. Follow the arrow down and go over the line you just made to the bottom line. Stop. That's lowercase d. Try it again.

Begin with your pencil on the number 1 at the top line and follow the arrow down to the bottom line. Pick up your pencil and put it on the number 2. Slant down to touch the first line you made. Follow the arrow and slant down to the bottom line. Stop. That's lowercase k. Try it again.

Begin with your pencil on the number 1, between the middle line and the bottom line, and follow the arrow across and then around in a circle. Stop a little above the bottom line. Stop. That's lowercase e. Try it again.

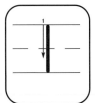

Begin with your pencil on the number 1 at the top line and follow the arrow down to the bottom line. Stop. That's lowercase l. Try it again.

Begin with your pencil on the number 1, just below the top line, and follow the arrow to curve up, touching the top line, then around and down, to the bottom line. Now pick up your pencil, put it on the number 2 at the middle line and go across the middle line. Stop. That's lowercase f. Try it again.

Begin with your pencil on the number 1 at the middle line and follow the arrow down to the bottom line. Without picking up your pencil, follow the arrow up and go over the line you just made. Just before you reach the middle line, curve around, touch the middle line and then go down to the bottom line. Go up to the middle line one more time, curve around and down to the bottom line. Stop. That's lowercase m. Try it again.

Begin with your pencil on the number 1 just below the middle line and follow the arrow to make a circle. Without picking up your pencil, continue up to the middle line and then follow the arrow down below the bottom line and curve up to make a little hook. Stop. That's lowercase g. Try it again.

Begin with your pencil on the number 1 at the middle line and follow the arrow down to the bottom line. Without picking up your pencil, follow the arrow up and go over the line you just made. Just before you reach the middle line, curve around, touch the middle line, and then go down to the bottom line. Stop. That's lowercase n. Try it again.

Scripts for Letter Formation

Lowercase Manuscript Letters, continued

Begin with your pencil on the number 1 just below the middle line and follow the arrow to make a circle. Stop. That's lowercase o. Try it again.

Begin with your pencil on the number 1 at the middle line and follow the arrow down. Curve around, touching the bottom line, and curve back up to the middle line. Without picking up your pencil, go down to the bottom line. Stop. That's lowercase u. Try it again.

Begin with your pencil on the number 1 at the middle line and follow the arrow down below the bottom line. Without picking up your pencil, go back up over the line you just made. Just before you reach the middle line, follow the arrow and curve up and around to make a circle. Stop. That's lowercase p. Try it again.

Begin with your pencil on the number 1 at the middle line and slant down to the bottom line. Without picking up your pencil, follow the arrow and slant up to the middle line. Stop. That's lowercase v. Try it again.

Begin with your pencil on the number 1 just below the middle line and follow the arrow to make a circle. Without picking up your pencil, continue up to the middle line and then follow the arrow down past the bottom line. Then make a little tail. Stop. That's lowercase q. Try it again.

Begin with your pencil on the number 1 at the middle line and slant down to the bottom line. Without picking up your pencil, follow the arrow and slant up to the middle line. Then follow the arrow and slant down to the bottom line. Follow the arrow one more time and slant up to the middle line. Stop. That's lowercase w. Try it again.

Begin with your pencil on the number 1 at the middle line and follow the arrow down to the bottom line. Without picking up your pencil, follow the arrow up and go over the line you just made. Just before you reach the middle line, curve up and around to make a hook. Stop. That's lowercase r. Try it again.

Begin with your pencil on the number 1 at the middle line and slant down to the bottom line. Pick up your pencil and put it on the number 2 at the middle line. Slant down to the bottom line, crossing the first line you drew. Stop. That's lowercase x. Try it again.

Begin with your pencil on the number 1 just below the middle line and follow the arrow to curve up, touch the middle line, then go round and around to the end of the curving line. Stop. That's lowercase s. Try it again.

Begin with your pencil on the number 1 at the middle line and slant down to the bottom line. Pick up your pencil and put it on the number 2 at the middle line and slant down, touching the first line you made. Continue down below the bottom line. Stop. That's lowercase y. Try it again.

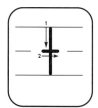

Begin with your pencil on the number 1 at the top line and follow the arrow down to the bottom line. Pick up your pencil and put it on the number 2 at the middle line. Go across the middle line. Stop. That's lowercase t. Try it again.

Begin with your pencil on the number 1 at the middle line and go across the middle line. Without picking up your pencil, slant down to the bottom line. Go across the bottom line. Stop. That's lowercase z. Try it again.

Scripts for Letter Formation

Uppercase Manuscript Letters

 Begin with your pencil on the number 1 at the top line and slant down to the bottom line. Pick up your pencil and put it on the number 2 at the top line and slant down to the bottom line. Pick up your pencil and put it on the number 3 and go across the middle line. Make sure you touch both lines you made. Stop. That's capital A. Try it again.

 Begin with your pencil on the number 1 at the top line and follow the arrow down to the bottom line. Now put your pencil on the number 2 at the top line and follow the arrow. Curve back in until you touch the first line you made. Then follow the next arrow. Curve back and follow the bottom line until you touch the first line you made. Stop. That's capital B. Try it again.

 Begin with your pencil on the number 1 just below the top line and go around in a circle, touching the top line and the bottom line as you curve around. Stop a little above the bottom line. That's capital C. Try it again.

 Begin with your pencil on the number 1 at the top line and follow the arrow down to the bottom line. Pick up your pencil and put it on the number 2. Follow the arrow down in a curve, to the first line you made. Stop. That's capital D. Try it again.

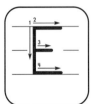 Begin with your pencil on the number 1 at the top line and follow the arrow down to the bottom line. Pick up your pencil and put it on the number 2. Go across the top line. Pick up your pencil and put it on the number 3 at the middle line. Go across the middle line. Then put your pencil on the number 4 at the bottom line and go across the bottom line. Stop. That's capital E. Try it again.

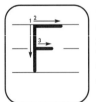 Begin with your pencil on the number 1 at the top line and follow the arrow down to the bottom line. Pick up your pencil and put it on the number 2. Go across the top line. Pick up your pencil and put it on the number 3. Go across the middle line. Stop. That's capital F. Try it again.

 Begin with your pencil on the number 1 just below the top line and go around in a circle, touching the top line and the bottom line as you curve around. Stop at the middle line. Without picking up your pencil, go across the middle line. Stop. That's capital G. Try it again.

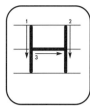 Begin with your pencil on the number 1 at the top line and follow the arrow down to the bottom line. Pick up your pencil and put it on the number 2 at the top line, and follow the arrow down to the bottom line. Lift your pencil and put it on the number 3 at the middle line. Go across the middle line, connecting both lines. Stop. That's capital H. Try it again.

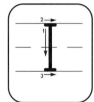 Begin with your pencil on the number 1 at the top line and go down to the bottom line. Pick up your pencil and put it on the number 2 at the top line and follow the arrow across the top line. Then put your pencil on the number 3 at the bottom line and go across the bottom line. Stop. That's capital I. Try it again.

 Begin with your pencil on the number 1 at the top line and follow the arrow down. Just before you get to the bottom line, curve around, touch the bottom line, and curve up to make a little hook. Pick up your pencil and put it on the number 2 at the top line. Go across the top line. Stop. That's capital J. Try it again.

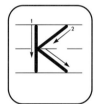 Begin with your pencil on the number 1 at the top line and follow the arrow down to the bottom line. Pick up your pencil and put it on the number 2 at the top line. Slant down to touch the first line you made at the middle line. Then slant down to the bottom line. Stop. That's capital K. Try it again.

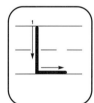 Begin with your pencil on the number 1 at the top line and follow the arrow down to the bottom line. Without picking up your pencil, go across the bottom line. Stop. That's capital L. Try it again.

 Begin with your pencil on the number 1 at the top line and follow the arrow down to the bottom line. Pick up your pencil, put it on the number 2 at the top line, and follow the arrow down to the bottom line. Without picking up your pencil, follow the arrow and slant up to the top line. Then follow the arrow down to the bottom line. Stop. That's capital M. Try it again.

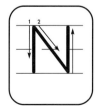 Begin with your pencil on the number 1 at the top line and follow the arrow down to the bottom line. Pick up your pencil and put it on the number 2 at the top line. Follow the arrow and slant down to the bottom line. Without picking up your pencil, follow the arrow straight up to the top line. Stop. That's capital N. Try it again.

Scripts for Letter Formation

Uppercase Manuscript Letters, continued

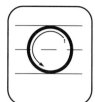 Begin with your pencil on the number 1 just below the top line and follow the arrow to make a circle. Touch the top line and the bottom line as you curve around to where you started. Stop. That's capital *O*. Try it again.

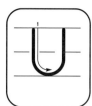 Begin with your pencil on the number 1 at the top line and follow the arrow down. Curve around, touch the bottom line, and curve back up to the top line. Stop. That's capital *U*. Try it again.

 Begin with your pencil on the number 1 at the top line and follow the arrow down to the bottom line. Now put your pencil on the number 2 at the top line and follow the arrow. Curve back in until you touch the first line you made. Stop. That's capital *P*. Try it again.

 Begin with your pencil on the number 1 at the top line and slant down to the bottom line. Without picking up your pencil, follow the arrow and slant up to the top line. Stop. That's capital *V*. Try it again.

 Begin with your pencil on the number 1 just below the top line and follow the arrow to make a circle. Touch the top line and the bottom line as you curve around to where you started. Pick up your pencil and put it on the number 2 between the middle line and the bottom line. Follow the arrow to make a short line to the bottom line. Stop. That's capital *Q*. Try it again.

 Begin with your pencil on the number 1 at the top line and slant down to the bottom line. Without picking up your pencil, follow the arrow and slant up to the top line. Then slant down to the bottom line. Now slant up to the top line one more time. Stop. That's capital *W*. Try it again.

 Begin with your pencil on the number 1 at the top line and follow the arrow down to the bottom line. Now put your pencil on the number 2 at the top line and follow the arrow. Curve back in until you touch the first line you made. Then, without picking up your pencil, slant down to the bottom line. Stop. That's capital *R*. Try it again.

 Begin with your pencil on the number 1 at the top line and slant down to the bottom line. Pick up your pencil and put it on the number 2 at the top line. Slant down to the bottom line, crossing the first line you made. Stop. That's capital *X*. Try it again.

 Begin with your pencil on the number 1 just below the top line and follow the arrow to curve up, touch the top line, then go round and around to the end of the curving line. Stop. That's capital *S*. Try it again.

 Begin with your pencil on the number 1 at the top line and slant down to the middle line. Pick up your pencil and put it on the number 2 at the top line, slant down to the middle line, touching the first line you made. Now go straight down to the bottom line. Stop. That's capital *Y*. Try it again.

 Begin with your pencil on the number 1 at the top line and follow the arrow down to the bottom line. Pick up your pencil, put it on the number 2 at the top line, and go across the top line. Stop. That's capital *T*. Try it again.

 Begin with your pencil on the number 1 at the top line and go across the top line. Without picking up your pencil, slant down to the bottom line, and then go across the bottom line. Stop. That's capital *Z*. Try it again.

Scripts for Letter Formation

Lowercase Cursive Letters

Begin with your pencil on the number 1 at the middle line and curve down to the bottom line. Touch the bottom line as you curve up to the number 2. Without picking up your pencil, follow the arrow down over the line you just made and touch the bottom line as you curve up to the middle line. Stop. That's lowercase *a*. Try it again.

Begin with your pencil on the number 1 at the bottom line and curve up to the top line. Before the top line, loop back and slant down to the bottom line at number 2. Without picking up your pencil, go over the line you just made and curve around to touch the middle line. Then slant down to touch the bottom line and curve up to the middle line. Stop. That's lowercase *h*. Try it again.

Begin with your pencil on the number 1 at the bottom line and curve up to the top line. Before the top line, loop back and slant down to the bottom line. Then touch the bottom line as you curve up to the number 2, at the middle line. Without picking up your pencil, swing out. Stop. That's lowercase *b*. Try it again.

Begin with your pencil on the number 1 at the bottom line and curve up to the middle line at number 2. Slant down to the bottom line and curve up to the middle line. Pick up your pencil, put it on the number 3, and make a dot. Stop. That's lowercase *i*. Try it again.

Begin with your pencil on the number 1 just below the middle line and follow the arrow down to make a little curve. Without picking up your pencil, follow the arrow as it curves up and around in a circle, touching the middle line and the bottom line as you curve around. Continue to curve up to the middle line. Stop. That's lowercase *c*. Try it again.

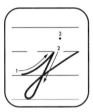

Begin with your pencil on the number 1 at the bottom line and curve up to the middle line at number 2. Slant all the way down below the bottom line. Loop back up to the line you just made and continue to the middle line. Lift up your pencil, put it on the number 3, and make a dot. Stop. That's lowercase *j*. Try it again.

Begin with your pencil on the number 1 at the middle line and curve down to the bottom line. Curve around to the number 1, touching the bottom line as you go around. Slant up to the number 2. Without picking up your pencil, go back over the line you just made and touch the bottom line as you curve up to the middle line. Stop. That's lowercase *d*. Try it again.

Begin with your pencil on the number 1 at the bottom line and slant up to the top line. Before the top line, loop back. Slant down to the bottom line to the number 2. Without picking up your pencil, go over the line you just made and curve around to touch the middle line. Then loop back to the first line you made, at number 3. Slant down to touch the bottom line and curve up to the middle line. Stop. That's lowercase *k*. Try it again.

Begin with your pencil on the number 1 at the bottom line and curve up to the middle line. Without picking up your pencil, loop back and slant down. Touch the bottom line as you curve up to the middle line. Stop. That's lowercase *e*. Try it again.

Begin with your pencil on the number 1 at the bottom line and curve up to the top line. Before the top line, loop back. Then slant down to the bottom line. Curve up to the middle line. Stop. That's lowercase *l*. Try it again.

Begin with your pencil on the number 1 at the bottom line. Slant up to the top line. Without picking up your pencil, loop back down, crossing your first line at the middle. Go all the way below the bottom line. Curve up to the number 2. Follow the arrow and swing up to the middle line. Stop. That's lowercase *f*. Try it again.

Begin with your pencil on the number 1 at the bottom line and curve up to the middle line. Then curve down to the number 2 at the bottom line. Without picking up your pencil, go over the line you just made and curve around to touch the middle line and then slant down to the number 3 at the bottom line. Now go over that line and curve around to touch the middle line and then slant down to the bottom line. Curve up once more to the middle line. Stop. That's lowercase *m*. Try it again.

Begin with your pencil on the number 1 at the middle line and curve down to the bottom line. Touch the bottom line as you curve up to the number 2. Without picking up your pencil, follow the arrow down over the line you just made and slant all the way down below the bottom line. Loop back up and continue to the middle line. Stop. That's lowercase *g*. Try it again.

Begin with your pencil on the number 1 at the bottom line and curve up to the middle line. Then curve down to the number 2 at the bottom line. Without picking up your pencil, go over the line you just made and curve around to touch the middle line and then slant down to the bottom line. Curve up once more to the middle line. Stop. That's lowercase *n*. Try it again.

Scripts for Letter Formation

Lowercase Cursive Letters, continued

 Begin with your pencil on the number 1 at the middle line and follow the arrow to make a circle, finishing at number 2 on the middle line. Without picking up your pencil, swing right to the middle line. Stop. That's lowercase *o*. Try it again.

 Begin with your pencil on the number 1 and curve up to the middle line at number 2. Slant all the way down, below the bottom line, and loop back to the middle line. Curve down in a circle, touching the bottom line and the last line you made at the number 3. Follow the arrow to curve up to the middle line. Stop. That's lowercase *p*. Try it again.

 Begin with your pencil on the number 1 at the middle line and curve down to the bottom line. Touch the bottom line and curve up to the number 2. Without picking up your pencil, follow the arrow and slant all the way down. Loop forward to the number 3 and then curve up to the middle line. Stop. That's lowercase *q*. Try it again.

 Begin with your pencil on the number 1 at the bottom line and curve up to the middle line. Without picking up your pencil, slant right from the number 2. Then slant down from the number 3 to the bottom line and curve up to the middle line. Stop. That's lowercase *r*. Try it again.

 Begin with your pencil on the number 1 at the bottom line and curve up to the middle line at number 2. Without picking up your pencil, curve down to the bottom line and curve in to the number 3, touching the first line you made. Now follow the arrow to curve up to the middle line. Stop. That's lowercase *s*. Try it again.

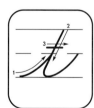 Begin with your pencil on the number 1 at the bottom line and curve up to the top line at number 2. Without picking up your pencil, slant down to the bottom line and then curve up to the middle line. Now pick up your pencil and put it on the number 3. Go across the first line you made. Stop. That's lowercase *t*. Try it again.

 Begin with your pencil on the number 1 at the bottom line and curve up to the middle line at number 2. Without picking up your pencil, slant down to the bottom line and curve up to the middle line at number 3. Slant down to the bottom line and curve up to the middle line once more. Stop. That's lowercase *u*. Try it again.

 Begin with your pencil on the number 1 at the bottom line and curve up to the middle line and then down to the bottom line. Curve up to the number 2 at the middle line. Without picking up your pencil, follow the arrow and swing right. Stop. That's lowercase *v*. Try it again.

 Begin with your pencil on the number 1 at the bottom line and curve up to the middle line at number 2. Without picking up your pencil, slant down to the bottom line and curve up to the number 3 at the middle line. Slant down to the bottom line and curve up to the number 4 at the middle line. Now follow the arrow to swing right. Stop. That's lowercase *w*. Try it again.

 Begin with your pencil on the number 1 at the bottom line and curve up to the middle line, then down to the bottom line, and up to the middle line once again. Pick up your pencil and put it on the number 2. Slant down to the bottom line. Stop. That's lowercase *x*. Try it again.

 Begin with your pencil on the number 1 at the bottom line and curve up to the middle line and then down to the bottom line. Curve up to the number 2 at the middle line and go down over that line, all the way down below the bottom line. Loop back and curve up to the middle line. Stop. That's lowercase *y*. Try it again.

 Begin with your pencil on the number 1 at the bottom line and curve up to the middle line and then down to the number 2 at the bottom line. Without picking up your pencil, go up a little then curve all the way down. Loop back and curve up to the middle line. Stop. That's lowercase *z*. Try it again.

Scripts for Letter Formation

Uppercase Cursive Letters

 Begin with your pencil on the number 1 at the top line and curve down to the bottom line. Touch the bottom line as you curve up to the number 2. Without picking up your pencil, follow the arrow down over the line you just made and touch the bottom line as you curve up to the middle line. Stop. That's capital *A*. Try it again.

 Begin with your pencil on the number 1 at the middle line and curve up to the top line at number 2. Slant down to the bottom line at number 3. Without picking up your pencil, retrace that line to the top line. Curve down to the middle line and make a loop. Curve down to the bottom line and continue to curve around to the number 4. Swing right. Stop. That's capital *B*. Try it again.

 Begin with your pencil on the number 1 at the top line and slant down a little to the number 2. Without picking up your pencil, follow the arrow as it curves up and around, touching the top line and the bottom line as you curve around to the middle line. Stop. That's capital *C*. Try it again.

 Begin with your pencil on the number 1 at the top line and curve down to the bottom line. Then curve up to make a loop. Curve down to the bottom line. Curve back to the number 1. Now, make another loop and swing right to the top line. Stop. That's capital *D*. Try it again.

 Begin with your pencil on the number 1 at the top line and slant down a little to the number 2. Without picking up your pencil, follow the arrow as it curves around to the middle line. Loop around the middle line and curve down again, touching the bottom line and continuing up a little more. Stop. That's capital *E*. Try it again.

 Begin with your pencil on the number 1 at the top line and slant down a little. Curve up at the number 2, then curve down a little and back up to the top line. Pick up your pencil and put it on the number 3. Curve down to the bottom line, touch the bottom line and curve up to the number 4. Follow the arrow and swing right. Pick up your pencil and put it on the number 5. Go across the middle line. Stop. That's capital *F*. Try it again.

 Begin with your pencil on the number 1 at the bottom line and slant up to the top line. Then loop down to the middle line and up to the number 2. Slant down to the bottom line and curve up to the middle line and the number 3. Swing right, crossing the first line you made. Stop. That's capital *G*. Try it again.

 Begin with your pencil on the number 1 at the top line, make a curve, and slant to the bottom line. Pick up your pencil and put it on the number 2 at the top line, make a curve, and slant to the bottom line at number 3. Without picking up your pencil, loop up to the middle line, touching the first line you made, and then loop back past the second line you made up to the middle line. Stop. That's capital *H*. Try it again.

 Begin with your pencil on the number 1 at the bottom line and curve up to the top line. Make a loop and curve down to the bottom line. Curve up to the number 2 at the middle line. Without picking up your pencil, swing right below the middle line. Stop. That's capital *I*. Try it again.

 Begin with your pencil on the number 1 at the bottom line and curve up to the top line. Make a loop and curve all the way down below the bottom line. Without picking up your pencil, loop back up to the middle line. Stop. That's capital *J*. Try it again.

 Begin with your pencil on the number 1 at the top line, make a curve, and slant to the bottom line. Pick up your pencil and put it on the number 2 at the top line. Curve down to the middle line, touching the first line you made at number 3. Slant down to the bottom line. Stop. That's capital *K*. Try it again.

 Begin with your pencil on the number 1 at the middle line and curve up to the top line. Loop back and slant down to the bottom line. Without picking up your pencil, loop and curve down below the bottom line and then up to the bottom line. Stop. That's capital *L*. Try it again.

 Begin with your pencil on the number 1 at the top line, make a curve, and slant to the number 2 at the bottom line. Without picking up your pencil, go over the line you just made and curve up past the middle line and then slant down to touch the number 3 at the bottom line. Now go over that line and curve past the middle line and then slant down to touch the bottom line. Stop. That's capital *M*. Try it again.

 Begin with your pencil on the number 1 at the top line, make a curve, and slant to the number 2 at the bottom line. Without picking up your pencil, go over the line you just made and curve up past the middle line and then slant down to touch the bottom line. Stop. That's capital *N*. Try it again.

© Hampton-Brown

Scripts for Letter Formation

Uppercase Cursive Letters, continued

Begin with your pencil on the number 1 at the top line and follow the arrow to make a circle. Loop back and swing right to the top line. Stop. That's capital *O*. Try it again.

Begin with your pencil on the number 1 at the top line and curve down to the bottom line. Curve up to the number 2 at the top line. Now go over that line to the bottom line. Stop. That's capital *U*. Try it again.

Begin with your pencil on the number 1 at the middle line and curve up to the top line at number 2. Slant down to the bottom line at number 3. Without picking up your pencil, go over that line to the top line and curve down in a circle to the middle line. Stop. That's capital *P*. Try it again.

Begin with your pencil on the number 1 at the top line and curve down to the bottom line. Curve up to the top line. Stop. That's capital *V*. Try it again.

Begin with your pencil on the number 1 at the bottom line and follow the arrow around to make a circle. Without picking up your pencil, loop back and curve down below the bottom line. Stop. That's capital *Q*. Try it again.

Begin with your pencil on the number 1 at the top line and curve down to the bottom line. Curve up to the number 2 at the top line. Without picking up your pencil, slant back down to the bottom line and then curve up to the top line. Stop. That's capital *W*. Try it again.

Begin with your pencil on the number 1 at the middle line and curve up to the top line at number 2. Slant down to the bottom line at number 3. Without picking up your pencil, go over that line to the top line and curve down in a circle to the middle line at number 4. Now slant down to the bottom line. Stop. That's capital *R*. Try it again.

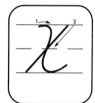

Begin with your pencil on the number 1 at the top line, curve down to the bottom line, and then curve up a little. Pick up your pencil and put it on the number 2. Slant down to the bottom line, crossing the first line you made. Stop. That's capital *X*. Try it again.

Begin with your pencil on the number 1 at the bottom line and curve up to the top line. Without picking up your pencil, loop back and curve down to the bottom line. Curve in. Cross the first line you made and continue to curve up to the number 2 at the middle line. Now swing right. Stop. That's capital *S*. Try it again.

Begin with your pencil on the number 1 at the top line and curve down to the bottom line. Curve up to the number 2 at the top line. Go over that line all the way down below the bottom line. Loop back and curve up to the middle line. Stop. That's capital *Y*. Try it again.

Begin with your pencil on the number 1 at the top line and slant down a little. Curve up at the number 2, then curve down a little and back up to the top line. Pick up your pencil and put it on the number 3. Curve down to the bottom line, touch the bottom line, and curve up to the number 4. Follow the arrow and swing right. Stop. That's capital *T*. Try it again.

Begin with your pencil on the number 1 at the top line. Curve down to the number 2. Without picking up your pencil, go up a little, then curve all the way down below the bottom line. Loop back up to the middle line. Stop. That's capital *Z*. Try it again.

Write the letters.

© Hampton-Brown

Write the letters.

N N N — — — — — — — — — — —

n n n — — — — — — — — — — —

L L L — — — — — — — — — — —

l l l — — — — — — — — — — —

P P P — — — — — — — — — — —

p p p — — — — — — — — — — —

G G G — — — — — — — — — — —

g g g — — — — — — — — — — —

I I I — — — — — — — — — — —

i i i — — — — — — — — — — —

Write the letters.

R R R - - - - - - - - - - - - - - - - - -

r r r - - - - - - - - - - - - - - - - - -

D D D - - - - - - - - - - - - - - - - - -

d d d - - - - - - - - - - - - - - - - - -

C C C - - - - - - - - - - - - - - - - - -

c c c - - - - - - - - - - - - - - - - - -

V V V - - - - - - - - - - - - - - - - - -

v v v - - - - - - - - - - - - - - - - - -

O O O - - - - - - - - - - - - - - - - - -

o o o - - - - - - - - - - - - - - - - - -

Write the letters.

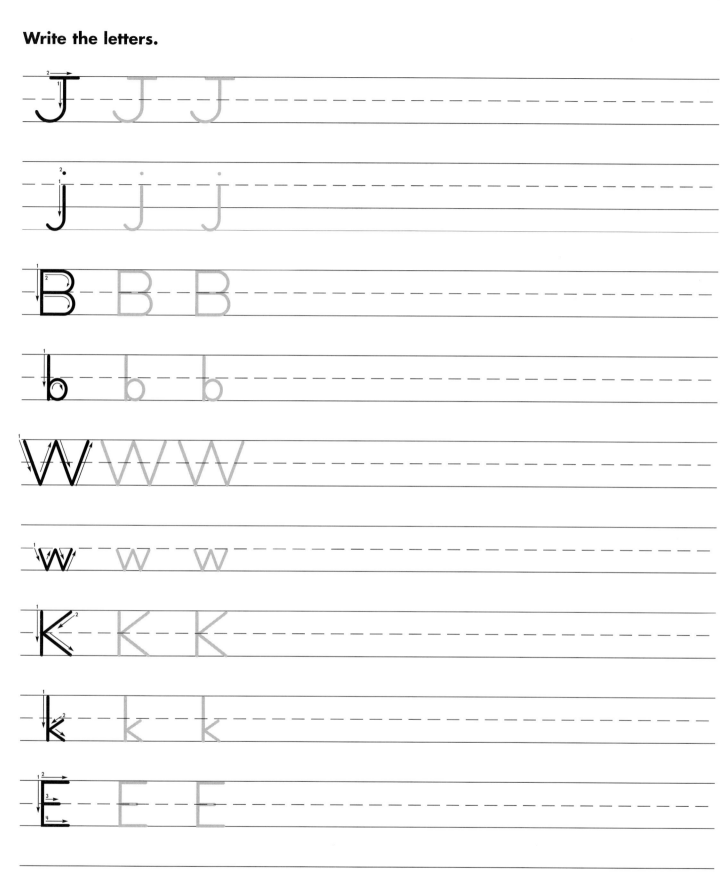

Write the letters.

Z Z Z

z z z

Y Y Y

y y y

U U U

u u u

Q Q Q

q q q

X X X

x x x

© Hampton-Brown

Write the letters.

Write the letters.

(handwriting practice: cursive letters n, m, L, t, P, p, G, g, l, N traced on ruled lines)

© Hampton-Brown

Write the letters.

R R R

N N N

D D D

d d d

C C C

v v v

U U U

N N N

O O O

o o o

Write the letters.

Write the letters.

Word Formation

Look at the words.

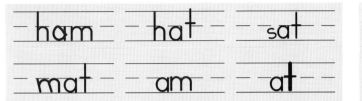

ham hat sat	ham hat sat
mat am at	mat am at
Not Correct	**Correct**

Trace each word. Then write it.

1. ham

2. hat

3. sat

4. mat

5. am

6. at

7. fat

8. Sam

Word Formation

Look at the words.

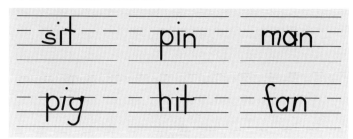

Not Correct

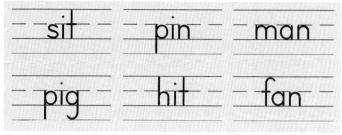

Correct

Trace each word. Then write it.

1. sit

2. pin

3. man

4. pig

5. hit

6. fan

7. it

8. an

Name _____   Date _____

Word Formation

Look at the words.

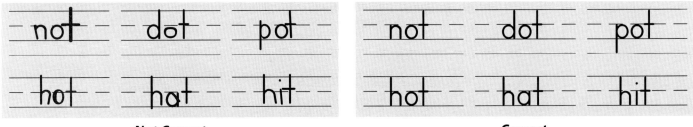

not   dot   pot
hot   hat   hit
Not Correct

not   dot   pot
hot   hat   hit
Correct

Trace each word. Then write it.

1. not

2. dot

3. pot

4. hot

5. hat

6. hit

7. on

8. in

© Hampton-Brown

Word Formation

Look at the words.

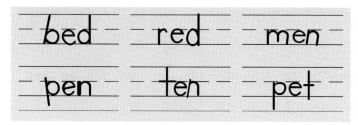

Not Correct	Correct

Trace each word. Then write it.

1. bed

2. red

3. men

4. pen

5. ten

6. pet

7. pat

8. pot

Word Formation

Look at the words.

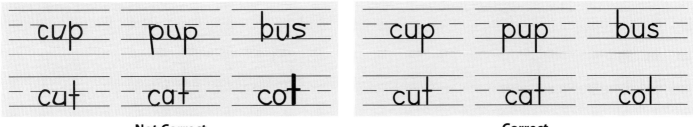

cup   pup   bus
cut   cat   cot
Not Correct

cup   pup   bus
cut   cat   cot
Correct

Trace each word. Then write it.

1. cup

2. pup

3. bus

4. cut

5. us

6. up

7. cat

8. cot

© Hampton-Brown

Word Formation

Look at the words.

| ham hat sat |
| mat am at |

Not Correct

| ham hat sat |
| mat am at |

Correct

Trace each word. Then write it.

1. *ham*

2. *hat*

3. *sat*

4. *mat*

5. *am*

6. *at*

7. *fat*

8. *Sam*

Name _____ Date _____

Word Formation

Look at the words.

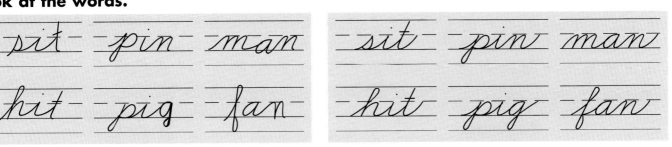

Not Correct   Correct

1. _sit_ _____

2. _pin_ _____

3. _man_ _____

4. _hit_ _____

5. _pig_ _____

6. _fan_ _____

7. _it_ _____

8. _an_ _____

© Hampton-Brown

Word Formation

Look at the words.

not	dot	pot
hot	hat	hit

Not Correct

not	dot	pot
hot	hat	hit

Correct

Trace each word. Then write it.

1. *not* _____ _____ _____ _____

2. *dot* _____ _____ _____ _____

3. *pot* _____ _____ _____ _____

4. *hot* _____ _____ _____ _____

5. *hat* _____ _____ _____ _____

6. *hit* _____ _____ _____ _____

7. *on* _____ _____ _____ _____

8. *in* _____ _____ _____ _____

Handwriting Practice 18
TE page T17b (for use after Transparency 6)

Name _____   Date _____

Word Formation

Look at the words.

| *bed* | *red* | *men* |
| *pen* | *ten* | *pet* |

Not Correct

| *bed* | *red* | *men* |
| *pen* | *ten* | *pet* |

Correct

Trace each word. Then write it.

1. *bed*

2. *red*

3. *men*

4. *pen*

5. *ten*

6. *pet*

7. *pat*

8. *pot*

© Hampton-Brown

Word Formation

Look at the words.

Not Correct

Correct

Trace each word. Then write it.

1. *cup*

2. *pup*

3. *bus*

4. *cut*

5. *us*

6. *cup*

7. *cat*

8. *cot*

Sentence Formation

Look at the statements.

Not Correct They are here. We can play.

Correct They are here. We can play.

Trace each statement. Then write it.

1. It is time for school. - - - - - - - - - - - - - - -

2. This food is good. - - - - - - - - - - - - - - -

3. They like my book. - - - - - - - - - - - - - - -

4. Here is the bed. - - - - - - - - - - - - - - -

5. Look at the time. - - - - - - - - - - - - - - -

6. Show the answer. - - - - - - - - - - - - - - -

7. I see the pig. - - - - - - - - - - - - - - -

8. The food is hot. - - - - - - - - - - - - - - -

© Hampton-Brown

Sentence Formation

Look at the question and answer.

Not Correct — What is your name? My name is Sam.

Correct — What is your name? My name is Sam.

Trace each question and answer. Then write them.

1. Who is she? That is Dot.

2. Do you like ham? No.

3. Are they here? Yes.

4. What is it? It is a pin.

5. Will you call? Yes, I will.

6. Can you see it? No.

7. How big is it? It is little.

8. Where is he? He is here.

© Hampton-Brown

Handwriting Practice 22
TE page T29b (for use after Lesson 52)

Sentence Formation

Look at the exclamations.

I think you are great!

Not Correct

I think you are great!

Correct

Trace each exclamation. Then write it.

1. This is so old!

2. I need help!

3. Don't do that!

4. She is great!

5. Look at the time!

6. You need to go!

7. Give me the book!

8. See you later!

© Hampton-Brown

Sentence Formation

Look at the statements.

Not Correct   *They are here. We can play.*

Correct   *They are here. We can play.*

Trace each statement. Then write it.

1. *It is time for school.*

2. *This food is good.*

3. *They like my book.*

4. *Here is the bed.*

5. *Look at the time.*

6. *Show the answer.*

7. *I see the pig.*

8. *The food is hot.*

Sentence Formation

Look at the question and answer.

Not Correct *What is your name? My name is Sam.*

Correct *What is your name? My name is Sam.*

Trace each question and answer. Then write them.

1. *Who is she? That is Dot.*

2. *Do you like ham? No.*

3. *Are they here? Yes.*

4. *What is it? It is a pin.*

5. *Will you call? Yes, I will.*

6. *Can you see it? No.*

7. *How big is it? It is little.*

8. *Where is he? He is here.*

Sentence Formation

Look at the exclamations.

I think you are great!

Not Correct

I think you are great!

Correct

Trace each exclamation. Then write it.

1. *This is so old!*

2. *I need help!*

3. *Don't do that!*

4. *She is great!*

5. *Look at the time!*

6. *You need to go!*

7. *Give me the book!*

8. *See you later!*

Manuscript Alphabet

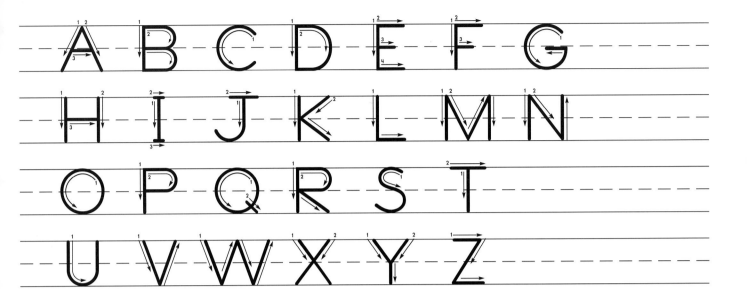

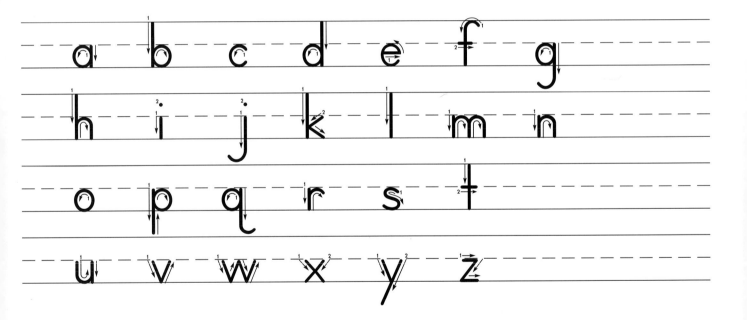

Cursive Alphabet

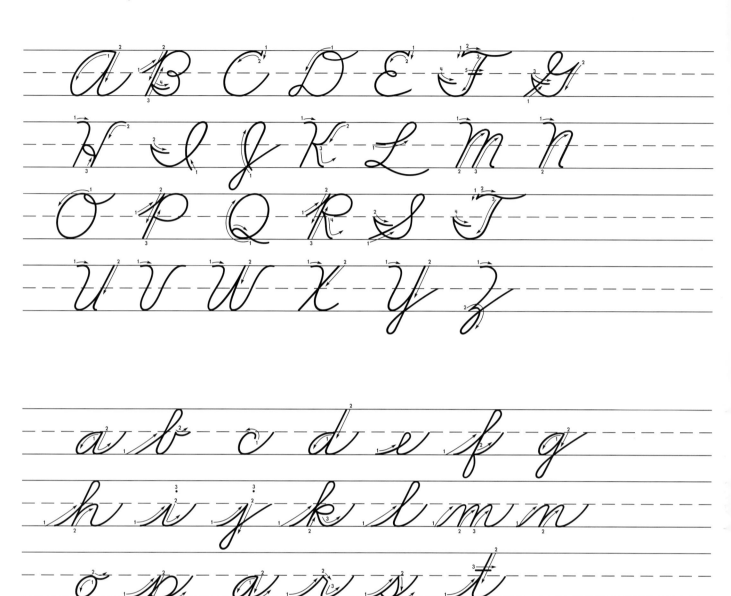

Handwriting Practice Sheet

Assessment
Materials

Language Acquisition Assessment

Purpose and Description

Lakeside School is designed for integrated instruction and assessment. It contains numerous opportunities for students to use language as they participate in authentic communicative activities. You can observe students during these activities to assess their progress in moving through the stages of language acquisition. The Language Acquisition Assessment facilitates the evaluation process because it

- identifies activities in which students will engage in the targeted language functions and will have natural opportunities to demonstrate the targeted patterns and structures
- identifies visuals that can be used to prompt language production.

Conducting the Language Acquisition Assessment

During the Language Acquisition Assessment, work with pairs and small groups of students so that the assessment process is manageable.

After the Language Acquisition Assessment, review the results to determine where students need additional instruction or support. Look for a pattern that might emerge. For example, for one student the "yes" boxes may be consistently marked in the Language Function sections, while in the Patterns and Structures sections, many of the boxes remain unchecked. This student needs more work on grammatical structures. You may wish to use another copy of the Language Acquisition Assessment pages to reassess these skills following additional instruction.

How to Use the Scoring Rubrics

Here, the teacher observed Kim and her partner as they role-played greeting each other, introducing a friend, and saying good-bye. Kim said *Hello. I am Kim. This is Marcos. Good-bye.* The teacher checked each box because Kim included all the key elements in her greetings, introductions, and good-byes.

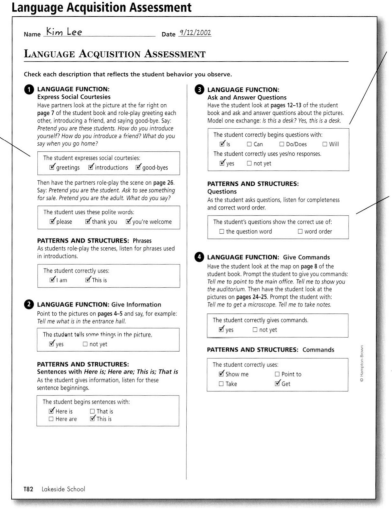

Language Acquisition Assessment

Name Kim Lee   Date 9/12/2002

LANGUAGE ACQUISITION ASSESSMENT

Check each description that reflects the student behavior you observe.

1 **LANGUAGE FUNCTION:**
Express Social Courtesies
Have partners look at the picture at the far right on **page 7** of the student book and role-play greeting each other, introducing a friend, and saying good-bye. Say: *Pretend you are these students. How do you introduce yourself? How do you introduce a friend? What do you say when you go home?*

The student expresses social courtesies:
☑ greetings   ☑ introductions   ☑ good-byes

Then have the partners role-play the scene on **page 26**. Say: *Pretend you are the student. Ask to see something for sale. Pretend you are the adult. What do you say?*

The student uses these polite words:
☑ please   ☑ thank you   ☑ you're welcome

PATTERNS AND STRUCTURES: Phrases
As students role-play the scenes, listen for phrases used in introductions.

The student correctly uses:
☑ I am   ☑ This is

2 **LANGUAGE FUNCTION: Give Information**
Point to the pictures on **pages 4–5** and say, for example: *Tell me what is in the entrance hall.*

The student tells some things in the picture.
☑ yes   ☐ not yet

PATTERNS AND STRUCTURES:
Sentences with *Here is; Here are; This is; That is*
As the student gives information, listen for these sentence beginnings.

The student begins sentences with:
☑ Here is   ☐ That is
☐ Here are   ☑ This is

3 **LANGUAGE FUNCTION:**
Ask and Answer Questions
Have the student look at **pages 12–13** of the student book and ask and answer questions about the pictures. Model one exchange: *Is this a desk? Yes, this is a desk.*

The student correctly begins questions with:
☑ Is   ☐ Can   ☐ Do/Does   ☐ Will
The student correctly uses yes/no responses.
☑ yes   ☐ not yet

PATTERNS AND STRUCTURES:
Questions
As the student asks questions, listen for completeness and correct word order.

The student's questions show the correct use of:
☐ the question word   ☐ word order

4 **LANGUAGE FUNCTION: Give Commands**
Have the student look at the map on **page 8** of the student book. Prompt the student to give you commands: *Tell me to point to the main office. Tell me to show you the auditorium.* Then have the student look at the pictures on **pages 24–25**. Prompt the student with: *Tell me to get a microscope. Tell me to take notes.*

The student correctly gives commands.
☑ yes   ☐ not yet

PATTERNS AND STRUCTURES: Commands

The student correctly uses:
☑ Show me   ☐ Point to
☐ Take   ☑ Get

© Hampton-Brown

T82   Lakeside School

Here, Kim was able to ask questions using *Is*, but was not able to ask questions with *Can, Do/Does*, or *Will*. The teacher marked the *Is* box. Kim successfully answered all the yes/no questions her partner asked her.

The teacher did not mark either box for Patterns and Structures because Kim was not able to use either pattern correctly.

This form shows that Kim needs additional instruction in asking questions beginning with *Can, Do/Does,* and *Will*. Once Kim has mastered these patterns, her use of language functions will improve.

Posttest

Purpose and Description

The Posttest measures students' cumulative knowledge of key vocabulary, language skills, reading, and writing learned in the course of the program.

Designed to familiarize students with standardized test formats, the Posttest includes multiple-choice items as well as short- and long-answer writing prompts. It includes five subtests:

1 Vocabulary Multiple-choice items test students' understanding of key vocabulary taught in *Lakeside School*. Students identify specific terms that apply to the pictures presented in the items.

2 Patterns and Structures This subtest uses multiple-choice format to test students' knowledge of English language patterns and structures taught in *Lakeside School*. In response to pictures, short questions, or sentence frames, students identify the appropriate English grammatical or structural elements.

3 Letter and Sound Correspondence This subtest assesses students' ability to associate a picture with a letter. Students look at a picture, say the name of the picture, and mark the letter that stands for the first sound.

4 Word Recognition Multiple-choice items assess students' recognition of high frequency sight words taught in *Lakeside School*. The teacher names a word for each item. Then students read a sentence and identify the dictated word in context.

5 Writing This subtest measures students' progress in writing skills and fluency. The prompts direct students to produce sentences in response to pictures related to *Lakeside School*.

Administering the Test

Assign the Posttest after students have completed *Lakeside School*. Make a copy of the test for each student. Read the directions aloud, and review the sample items with the students. Students should not use their books during the test. Use this script for the Word Recognition Subtest.

WORD RECOGNITION

For the Sample, say:
Read the sentence. Fill in the circle under the word **have**. *The word is* **have**.

For Items 70–91, say:
Read the sentence for number ___. Fill in the circle under the word ___. The word is ___.

70. me	76. later	82. my	88. things
71. here	77. can	83. girl	89. think
72. great	78. not	84. no	90. year
73. around	79. work	85. she	91. time
74. good	80. for	86. which	
75. point	81. read	87. put	

Scoring the Test

The Posttest is scored on a 100-point scale. The Answer Key below provides the answers to all multiple-choice test items as well as rubrics for scoring written responses. Score each subtest using the scoring system indicated in the Answer Key. Record the score for each student at the top of the first page of the test.

Using Test Results

You can use the results of the Posttest to assist you, students, and their families in evaluating students' progress and defining instructional goals.

ANSWER KEY

VOCABULARY
(23 points — 1 point each)

1. H	6. B	11. J	16. C	21. H
2. A	7. F	12. B	17. G	22. B
3. F	8. D	13. J	18. C	23. J
4. A	9. G	14. B	19. J	
5. H	10. A	15. F	20. B	

PATTERNS AND STRUCTURES
(15 points — 1 point each)

24. F	27. D	30. H	33. C	36. F
25. A	28. F	31. A	34. J	37. A
26. H	29. A	32. F	35. C	38. J

LETTERS AND SOUNDS
(31 points — 1 point each)

39. b	46. c	53. r	60. o	67. G
40. f	47. t	54. w	61. i	68. C
41. m	48. h	55. a	62. e	69. G
42. p	49. k	56. y	63. qu	
43. z	50. j	57. g	64. x	
44. d	51. s	58. n	65. G	
45. l	52. v	59. u	66. A	

WORD RECOGNITION
(22 points — 1 point each)

70. G	75. A	80. G	85. B	90. J
71. D	76. J	81. B	86. F	91. D
72. J	77. B	82. G	87. C	
73. B	78. G	83. B	88. G	
74. H	79. B	84. F	89. A	

WRITING
(9 points — 3 points each)

Award points based on the following criteria:

92. 2 points for a sentence that tells about the picture.
   1/2 point for capitalizing the first word of the sentence.
   1/2 point for a period at the end of the sentence.

93. 2 points for a question about the picture.
   1/2 point for capitalizing the first word of the question.
   1/2 point for a question mark at the end of the question.

94. 2 points for an exclamation related to the picture.
   1/2 point for capitalizing the first word of the sentence.
   1/2 point for an exclamation point at the end of the sentence.

Name _____ Date _____

LANGUAGE ACQUISITION ASSESSMENT

Check each description that reflects the student behavior you observe.

① LANGUAGE FUNCTION:
Express Social Courtesies
Have partners look at the picture at the far right on **page 7** of the student book and role-play greeting each other, introducing a friend, and saying good-bye. Say: *Pretend you are these students. How do you introduce yourself? How do you introduce a friend? What do you say when you go home?*

> The student expresses social courtesies:
> ☐ greetings ☐ introductions ☐ good-byes

Then have the partners role-play the scene on **page 26**. Say: *Pretend you are the student. Ask to see something for sale. Pretend you are the adult. What do you say?*

> The student uses these polite words:
> ☐ please ☐ thank you ☐ you're welcome

PATTERNS AND STRUCTURES: Phrases
As students role-play the scenes, listen for phrases used in introductions.

> The student correctly uses:
> ☐ I am ☐ This is

② LANGUAGE FUNCTION: Give Information
Point to the pictures on **pages 4–5** and say, for example: *Tell me what is in the entrance hall.*

> The student tells some things in the picture.
> ☐ yes ☐ not yet

PATTERNS AND STRUCTURES:
Sentences with *Here is; Here are; This is; That is*
As the student gives information, listen for these sentence beginnings.

> The student begins sentences with:
> ☐ Here is ☐ That is
> ☐ Here are ☐ This is

③ LANGUAGE FUNCTION:
Ask and Answer Questions
Have the student look at **pages 12–13** of the student book and ask and answer questions about the pictures. Model one exchange: *Is this a desk? Yes, this is a desk.*

> The student correctly begins questions with:
> ☐ Is ☐ Can ☐ Do/Does ☐ Will
> The student correctly uses yes/no responses.
> ☐ yes ☐ not yet

PATTERNS AND STRUCTURES:
Questions
As the student asks questions, listen for completeness and correct word order.

> The student's questions show the correct use of:
> ☐ the question word ☐ word order

④ LANGUAGE FUNCTION: Give Commands
Have the student look at the map on **page 8** of the student book. Prompt the student to give you commands: *Tell me to point to the main office. Tell me to show you the auditorium.* Then have the student look at the pictures on **pages 24–25**. Prompt the student with: *Tell me to get a microscope. Tell me to take notes.*

> The student correctly gives commands.
> ☐ yes ☐ not yet

PATTERNS AND STRUCTURES: Commands

> The student correctly uses:
> ☐ Show me ☐ Point to
> ☐ Take ☐ Get

LANGUAGE ACQUISITION ASSESSMENT, continued

Check each description that reflects the student behavior you observe.

5 LANGUAGE FUNCTION:
Ask For and Give Information
Have the student look at **pages 16–17** of the student book. Ask the student questions about the pictures. Say: *What does this girl have?* If the student responds with one word or a phrase, say: *Use a complete sentence.*

> The student supplies appropriate information.
> ☐ yes   ☐ not yet

Then have the student ask you questions about the picture.

> The student correctly asks for information.
> ☐ yes   ☐ not yet

PATTERNS AND STRUCTURES:
Pronouns; Present Tense Verbs *(has, have)*
As the student asks for and gives information, listen for pronouns and verbs.

> The student correctly uses:
> ☐ she   ☐ has
> ☐ he   ☐ have
> ☐ they

6 LANGUAGE FUNCTION:
Express Needs and Feelings
Have the student look at **pages 20–21** in the student book. Point to several pictures and say: *Pretend you are this student. Tell what you need. Tell what you need to do. Tell how you feel.* If the student responds with one word or a phrase, say: *Use a complete sentence.*

> The student expresses needs and feelings.
> ☐ yes   ☐ not yet

PATTERNS AND STRUCTURES: Pronoun *I*

As the student expresses needs and feelings, listen for the pronoun *I*.

> The student correctly uses:
> ☐ I need   ☐ I need to   ☐ I feel

7 LANGUAGE FUNCTION: Express Likes and Dislikes
Have the student look at **pages 22–23** of the student book and state likes and dislikes as they point out and name three specific foods. Say: *Tell me which food you like. Tell me which food you do not like.* If the student simply names food items, say: *Use a complete sentence.*

> The student expresses likes and dislikes.
> ☐ yes   ☐ not yet

PATTERNS AND STRUCTURES:
Positive and Negative Statements
As the student expresses likes and dislikes, listen for positive and negative statements.

> The student correctly uses:
> ☐ I like   ☐ I do not like

8 LANGUAGE FUNCTION: Describe Actions
Use the pictures on **pages 18–19** of the student book. Have the student point to three different pictures and describe the actions they see. Say: *What does she do? What does he do?*

> The student correctly describes actions.
> ☐ yes   ☐ not yet

PATTERNS AND STRUCTURES:
Third Person Action Verbs with *-s*
As the student describes actions, listen for verbs.

> The student uses *-s* at the end of third-person action verbs. For example: *She plays. He runs.*
> ☐ yes   ☐ not yet

Vocabulary *(23 points — 1 point each)*

 Closed Book

DIRECTIONS Find the word that names the picture. Mark your answer.

Sample

- Ⓐ gym
- Ⓑ field
- Ⓒ fence
- Ⓓ bench

1
- Ⓕ flag
- Ⓖ window
- Ⓗ front door
- Ⓙ room number

2
- Ⓐ desk
- Ⓑ ruler
- Ⓒ paper
- Ⓓ notebook

3
- Ⓕ stapler
- Ⓖ scissors
- Ⓗ highlighter
- Ⓙ microscope

4
- Ⓐ main office
- Ⓑ nurse's office
- Ⓒ janitor's closet
- Ⓓ boy's bathroom

5
- Ⓕ library
- Ⓖ hallway
- Ⓗ cafeteria
- Ⓙ auditorium

6
- Ⓐ math class
- Ⓑ science class
- Ⓒ reading class
- Ⓓ social studies class

7
- Ⓕ eight thirty
- Ⓖ nine thirty
- Ⓗ eight o'clock
- Ⓙ eight forty-five

8
- Ⓐ ten thirty
- Ⓑ eleven fifteen
- Ⓒ twelve o'clock
- Ⓓ eleven o'clock

9
- Ⓕ I observe.
- Ⓖ I raise my hand.
- Ⓗ I do an experiment.
- Ⓙ I work with a group.

10
- Ⓐ circle
- Ⓑ square
- Ⓒ triangle
- Ⓓ rectangle

11
- Ⓕ floor
- Ⓖ mailbox
- Ⓗ computer
- Ⓙ telephone

© Hampton-Brown

GO ON

Vocabulary, continued

12
- Ⓐ ceiling
- Ⓑ calendar
- Ⓒ bulletin board
- Ⓓ copy machine

13
- Ⓕ printer
- Ⓖ keyboard
- Ⓗ newspaper
- Ⓙ encyclopedia

14
- Ⓐ track
- Ⓑ soccer
- Ⓒ softball
- Ⓓ basketball

15
- Ⓕ ear
- Ⓖ eye
- Ⓗ hair
- Ⓙ elbow

16
- Ⓐ ankle
- Ⓑ throat
- Ⓒ stomach
- Ⓓ shoulder

17
- Ⓕ cake
- Ⓖ soup
- Ⓗ bagel
- Ⓙ salad

18
- Ⓐ taco
- Ⓑ hot dog
- Ⓒ hamburger
- Ⓓ cottage cheese

19
- Ⓕ apple
- Ⓖ grape
- Ⓗ orange
- Ⓙ banana

20
- Ⓐ dime
- Ⓑ nickel
- Ⓒ penny
- Ⓓ quarter

21
- Ⓕ one dollar
- Ⓖ two dollars
- Ⓗ five dollars
- Ⓙ ten dollars

22
- Ⓐ socks
- Ⓑ shorts
- Ⓒ sneakers
- Ⓓ sweatpants

23
- Ⓕ cap
- Ⓖ T-shirt
- Ⓗ jacket
- Ⓙ sweatshirt

GO ON

Patterns and Structures *(15 points — 1 point each)*

DIRECTIONS Look at each picture. What words are missing?
Mark your answer.

Sample

Ⓐ is it
Ⓑ am I
Ⓒ I am
Ⓓ you are

25

Ⓐ Here is
Ⓑ Can you
Ⓒ They have
Ⓓ Where are

24

Ⓕ This is
Ⓖ You are
Ⓗ Here are
Ⓙ What time

26

Ⓕ Is this some
Ⓖ Are some here
Ⓗ Here are some
Ⓙ Some are here

GO ON

© Hampton-Brown

Patterns and Structures, continued

27

Room 118?

(A) Do you
(B) Can he
(C) Does this
(D) Where is

29

Do you like hot dogs?

No, ___ ___ ___ ___ hot dogs.

(A) I do not like
(B) I like not the
(C) I not like the
(D) not I like those

28

What time is it?

11 o'clock.

(F) It is
(G) It has
(H) It does
(J) That is

30

Who has a newspaper?

___ ___ a newspaper.

(F) He is
(G) You can
(H) She has
(J) She can

GO ON

© Hampton-Brown

Patterns and Structures, continued

31

— — the teacher?

He is Mr. Duncan.

- Ⓐ Who is
- Ⓑ Will you
- Ⓒ Who are
- Ⓓ How does

32

This is the problem.

— — the answer?

- Ⓕ What is
- Ⓖ Do they
- Ⓗ Are they
- Ⓙ What are

33

— — — make a call.

- Ⓐ I like this
- Ⓑ This is in
- Ⓒ I need to
- Ⓓ She does not

34

How does your mom feel?

— — — .

- Ⓕ He feel fine.
- Ⓖ He feels fine.
- Ⓗ She feel fine.
- Ⓙ She feels fine.

 GO ON

Patterns and Structures, continued

35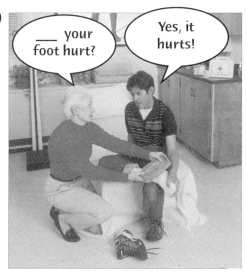

"___ your foot hurt?"

"Yes, it hurts!"

Ⓐ Do
Ⓑ Can
Ⓒ Does
Ⓓ What

36

"___ ___ ___ to dance?"

"Yes, I like to dance."

Ⓕ Do you like
Ⓖ Do you likes
Ⓗ Does you like
Ⓙ Does you likes

37

"Can you see it?"

"Yes, __ __ see it."

Ⓐ I can
Ⓑ I have
Ⓒ I think
Ⓓ Point to

38

"Carlos ___ softball."

Ⓕ run
Ⓖ like
Ⓗ sings
Ⓙ plays

GO ON

Letters and Sounds *(31 points — 1 point each)*

DIRECTIONS Say the name of the picture. Find the letter that spells the <u>first</u> sound. Mark your answer.

Sample

- ○ h
- ● k
- ○ y

39
- ○ m
- ○ b
- ○ t

40
- ○ f
- ○ v
- ○ s

41
- ○ v
- ○ l
- ○ m

42
- ○ p
- ○ b
- ○ z

43
- ○ r
- ○ z
- ○ c

44
- ○ t
- ○ w
- ○ d

45
- ○ l
- ○ r
- ○ u

46
- ○ c
- ○ d
- ○ e

47
- ○ f
- ○ t
- ○ g

48
- ○ d
- ○ o
- ○ h

49
- ○ k
- ○ y
- ○ g

50
- ○ j
- ○ w
- ○ k

51
- ○ s
- ○ d
- ○ i

52
- ○ p
- ○ h
- ○ v

53
- ○ l
- ○ r
- ○ m

54
- ○ m
- ○ h
- ○ w

55
- ○ o
- ○ a
- ○ e

56
- ○ w
- ○ e
- ○ y

57
- ○ k
- ○ j
- ○ g

GO ON →

Letters and Sounds, continued

58
- ○ n
- ○ g
- ○ m

59
- ○ e
- ○ u
- ○ t

60
- ○ f
- ○ o
- ○ a

61
- ○ i
- ○ r
- ○ e

62
- ○ i
- ○ e
- ○ s

DIRECTIONS Say the name of the picture. Find the letters that spell the **first two** sounds. Mark your answer.

63
- ○ qa
- ○ wu
- ○ qu

DIRECTIONS Say the name of the picture. Find the letter that spells the **last two** sounds. Mark your answer.

64
- ○ c
- ○ x
- ○ z

DIRECTIONS Which word names the picture? Mark your answer.

> ### Sample
>
>
> - Ⓐ man
> - Ⓑ mop
> - Ⓒ map

65
- Ⓕ hit
- Ⓖ hat
- Ⓗ hot

66
- Ⓐ pin
- Ⓑ pan
- Ⓒ pen

67
- Ⓕ cap
- Ⓖ cup
- Ⓗ cut

68
- Ⓐ pit
- Ⓑ pat
- Ⓒ pot

69
- Ⓕ bad
- Ⓖ bed
- Ⓗ red

GO ON ➡

Word Recognition *(22 points — 1 point each)*

DIRECTIONS Find the word your teacher reads. Mark your answer.

Sample

They have an old cat.
Ⓐ ● Ⓑ   Ⓒ Ⓓ

70 Give me an answer.
Ⓕ Ⓖ Ⓗ   Ⓙ

71 How can I help here?
Ⓐ   Ⓑ Ⓒ   Ⓓ

72 We do feel great!
Ⓕ Ⓖ Ⓗ   Ⓙ

73 Boys and girls help around that school.
        Ⓐ   Ⓑ   Ⓒ   Ⓓ

74 Take some good food.
Ⓕ   Ⓖ   Ⓗ   Ⓙ

75 Point to a picture you like.
Ⓐ Ⓑ   Ⓒ   Ⓓ

76 Write those letters later.
Ⓕ   Ⓖ   Ⓗ   Ⓙ

77 He can call me tomorrow.
Ⓐ Ⓑ Ⓒ   Ⓓ

78 Do not show me the number.
Ⓕ Ⓖ Ⓗ   Ⓙ

79 Who can work with them?
Ⓐ   Ⓑ   Ⓒ   Ⓓ

80 These are for both of us.
        Ⓕ Ⓖ Ⓗ Ⓙ

81 I need to read a book she has.
Ⓐ   Ⓑ   Ⓒ   Ⓓ

82 They like my name, too.
Ⓕ   Ⓖ   Ⓗ   Ⓙ

83 Can the little girl get a pet soon?
        Ⓐ Ⓑ Ⓒ   Ⓓ

84 No, I don't see them at night.
Ⓕ   Ⓖ   Ⓗ   Ⓙ

85 Yes, she does like you.
Ⓐ Ⓑ Ⓒ   Ⓓ

86 Which boy will play?
Ⓕ   Ⓖ   Ⓗ Ⓙ

87 Where did he put it?
Ⓐ   Ⓑ   Ⓒ Ⓓ

88 These things look very good.
Ⓕ   Ⓖ   Ⓗ   Ⓙ

89 I think this is a hot day.
Ⓐ Ⓑ Ⓒ   Ⓓ

90 What can your group do in a year?
Ⓕ   Ⓖ   Ⓗ Ⓙ

91 The bus is not on time.
Ⓐ   Ⓑ Ⓒ Ⓓ

GO ON ➤

Writing *(9 points — 3 points each)*

DIRECTIONS Read each item and look at the picture. Write your answers.

92 Write a sentence to tell about this picture.

_____

_____

_____

_____

93 Write a question about this picture.

_____

_____

_____

_____

94 Write an exclamation to tell about this picture.

_____

_____

_____

_____

STOP

Cooperative Learning Strategies

Lakeside School activities make use of the following basic cooperative-learning structures.

STRUCTURE & GRAPHIC	DESCRIPTION	BENEFITS & PURPOSES
INSIDE-OUTSIDE CIRCLE	• Students stand in concentric circles facing each other. • Students in the outside circle ask questions; those inside answer. • On a signal, students rotate to create new partnerships. • On another signal, students trade inside/outside roles.	• Talking one-on-one with a variety of partners gives risk-free practice in speaking skills. • Interactions can be structured to focus on specific speaking skills. • Students practice both speaking and active listening.
THINK, PAIR, SHARE Think A B Pair A B Share A B	• Students think about a topic suggested by the teacher. • Pairs discuss the topic. • Students individually share information with the class.	• The opportunity for self-talk during individual think time allows the student to formulate thoughts before speaking. • Discussion with a partner reduces performance anxiety and enhances understanding.